MORE
BIBLE
ACTIVITIES

Written by
Ken & Vickie Save

Illustrated by
Ken Save

BARBOUR BOOKS
An Imprint of Barbour Publishing, Inc.

© MCMXCIX by Barbour Publishing, Inc.

ISBN 1-57748-597-1

Published by Barbour Books, an imprint of Barbour Publishing, Inc., P.O. Box 719, Uhrichsville, Ohio 44683, www.barbourbooks.com

ecpa Member of the
Evangelical Christian
Publishers Association

Printed in the United States of America.
5 4 3

MORE
BIBLE
ACTIVITIES

COLOR *the* PICTURE

LET'S FOLLOW JESUS

SOME DAYS LIFE CAN BE REALLY TOUGH. WE CAN HAVE PROBLEMS AT SCHOOL, WITH OUR FREINDS, AT HOME, AND EVEN WITH OUR PARENTS.

SOME DAYS WE CAN FEEL REALLY ANGRY OR AFRAID OR HURT OR LONELY — AND THAT'S ONLY A FEW OF THE FEELINGS WE WILL EXPERIENCE AS WE GROW THROUGH LIFE.

SO WHAT DO WE DO? HOW DO WE HANDLE ALL OUR FEELINGS? HOW DO WE HANDLE THE PROBLEMS THAT CAN COME AND BRING UP THESE FEELINGS IN US?

DO WE HAVE A CHOICE IN HOW WE CAN HANDLE OUR PROBLEMS AND FEELINGS?

YES! THERE IS A WAY: IF WE TURN TO GOD AND ASK HIM FOR HELP, HE CAN TEACH US HOW TO HANDLE SITUATIONS THAT WILL LEAD US TO HAVE HAPPIER LIVES.

IT'S A BETTER WAY, IF WE FOLLOW JESUS.

LET'S FIND OUT HOW!

"I AM THE LIGHT OF THE WORLD. WHOEVER FOLLOWS ME WILL NEVER WALK IN DARKNESS, BUT WILL HAVE THE LIGHT OF LIFE."

JOHN 8:12

WORD SEARCH

FEELINGS, FEELINGS—EVERYWHERE ARE FEELINGS!

FIND THE FEELINGS LISTED BELOW IN THE WORD SEARCH ON THE NEXT PAGE.

JOY

HURT

ANGER

LOVE

HATRED

FEAR

LONELINESS

PRIDE

GUILT

PEACE

HAPPINESS

WORRY

```
H R Q L Y V D M F K F W
F J G O N C L G P E F B
G S J V B T B X B W A L
A D B E B D F L X O T R
P N T P E L Q S C R F D
T P G R B W C X U R S X
R Z T E B V D H V Y S G
W A C T R B D M D M E W
H A P P I N E S S P N L
Q L R V B J D Z B D I D
M W I B B P E K C F L Q
B Y D N B C T W T H E J
T C E P A Q N S N K N W
N M J E B V S M Q B O P
K R P D B R D G U I L T
```

FILL *in the* BLANKS

SO MANY FEELINGS, SO MANY PROBLEMS. GOOD TIMES, BAD TIMES. HAPPINESS, DISAPPOINTMENT. IT'S CONFUSING! HOW DO YOU COPE—HOW DO YOU SORT IT ALL OUT?

LOOK TO GOD AND REALLY PUT YOUR TRUST IN **HIM**. NOT ONLY WILL YOU HAVE A GUARANTEE OF HEAVEN ONE DAY, BUT **HE** WILL HELP YOU RIGHT NOW AND IN EVERY DAY AHEAD!

GRACE   THRONE
CONFIDENCE   HELP
TIME   MERCY
APPROACH   NEED
RECEIVE

USING THE WORDS ABOVE, COMPLETE THE VERSE ON THE NEXT PAGE.

"LET US THEN _____
THE _____ OF GRACE WITH
_____, SO THAT WE MAY
_____ _____ AND FIND
_____ TO _____ US IN OUR
_____ OF _____."

HEBREWS 4:16

SCRAMBLED VERSES

WHAT DID JESUS SAY?

UNSCRAMBLE THE VERSE BELOW AND COMPLETE THE NEXT PAGE TO READ JESUS' OWN WORDS TO YOU!

"EOCM OT EM, LAL OYU OWH REA YWRAE NAD DNEEBRUD, DAN I LILW EGVI UYO ETSR. ETKA YM YEKO PNUO UYO NAD RLNAE MFOR EM, RFO I MA NTGELE DNA MUHLBE NI ARTHE, ADN UOY LIWL IDFN SRTE OFR ROYU SSLUO. RFO MY KYEO SI SYAE DAN MY UDBERN SI ITLGH."

"———— —— ——,
—— —— —— ——— —— ———
——— ——————— —— ———
—————————, ———
— ——— ——— ———
——— ———. ———
—— —— ——— ———
—— — ——— ———————
———— ——, ——— —
—— ——————— —— ———
—— ——— ——— ———
————, ——— ———
——— ——— ——— ———
—— ——— ——— ———————.
—— ——— ——— —— ———
————— ——— ——— ———-
—— —— —— ———— ——."

SECRET CODES

JESUS SAVES!

TO SOLVE THE CODED VERSE BELOW, LOOK AT EACH LETTER AND WRITE THE ONE THAT COMES BEFORE IT IN THE ALPHABET.

"GPS UIF XBHFT PG TJO JT EFBUI, CVU UIF HJGU PG HPE JT FUFSOBM MJGF JO DISJTU KFTVT PVS MPSE."

A B C D E F G H I J K L M N O P Q R S
T U V W X Y Z

"___ ___ ___   ___ ___ ___   ___ ___ ___ ___

___ ___   ___ ___ ___   ___ ___

___ ___ ___ ___ ___,   ___ ___ ___

___ ___ ___ ___ ___ ___ ___   ___ ___

___ ___ ___   ___ ___   ___ ___ ___ ___-

___ ___ ___   ___ ___   ___ ___ ___

___ ___ ___ ___ ___   ___ ___ ___ ___

___ ___ ___   ___ ___ ___ ___."

ROMANS 6:23

13

FINISH *the* VERSE

NEW LIFE!

WHEN YOU TRUST IN GOD, HIS SPIRIT WILL GIVE YOU THE DESIRE AND THE STRENGTH TO MAKE THE RIGHT CHOICES IN YOUR LIFE. ALL YOU NEED TO DO IS ASK HIM!

USE THE CODE CHART BELOW TO FINISH THE VERSE. (EG: K=24)

	1	2	3	4	5	6	7
1	A	B	C	D	E	F	G
2	H	I	J	K	L	M	N
3	O	P	Q	R	S	T	U
4	V	W	X	Y	Z		

"SO I ___ ___ ___, ___ ___ ___ ___
       35 11 44   25 22 41 15

BY THE ___ ___ ___ ___ ___ ___,   AND
        35 32 22 34 22 36

YOU   ___ ___ ___ ___   NOT
         42 22 25 25

         THE

___ ___ ___ ___ ___ ___ ___
17 34 11 36 22 16 44

___ ___ ___ ___ ___ ___ ___   OF THE
14 15 35 22 34 15 35

___ ___ ___ ___ ___ ___   ___ ___ ___ ___ ___ ___."
35 22 27 16 37 25   27 11 36 37 34 15

                                    GALATIANS 5:16

FILL THEM IN

FRUIT OF THE SPIRIT

LOOK UP GALATIANS 5:22-23 IN YOUR BIBLE.

ON THE NEXT PAGE, FILL IN THE BOXES WITH THE FRUIT OF THE SPIRIT.

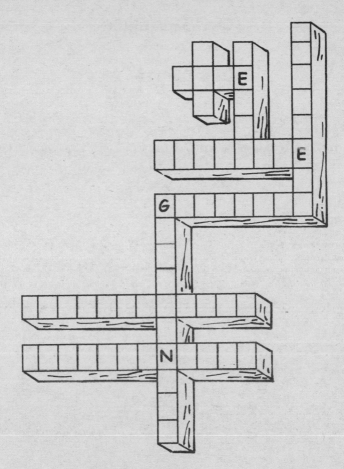

CROSSWORD

ANGER

ANGER CAN BE A PRETTY AWFUL FEELING. OVER THE NEXT FEW PAGES, LET'S SEE WHAT GOD SAYS ABOUT ANGER AND HOW WE CAN FIND HELP TO HANDLE ANGER.

ACROSS

1. "MY DEAR _____, TAKE NOTE OF THIS."
2. "_____ SHOULD BE QUICK TO LISTEN."
3. "SLOW TO _____,"
4. "AND _____ TO BECOME ANGRY."

DOWN

1. "FOR MAN'S _____."
2. "DOES NOT _____ ABOUT."
3. "THE _____ LIFE."
4. "THAT ____ DESIRES."

JAMES 1:19-20

19

DOUBLE *the* FUN

UNSCRAMBLE THE UNDERLINED WORDS IN
EACH VERSE. ON THE NEXT PAGE, PLACE YOUR
ANSWERS IN THE SPACES PROVIDED AND
THEN COMPLETE THE CROSSWORD PUZZLE.

1. "IN YOUR ANGER DO NOT SIN; WHEN YOU
ARE ON YOUR DESB, SEARCH YOUR ATRHSE
AND BE SILENT."

PSALM 4:4

2. "FOR HIS ENARG LASTS ONLY A TMOENM,
BUT HIS FAVOR LASTS A LIFETIME."

PSALM 30:5

3. "YET HE WAS MERCIFUL; HE VROEAFG
THEIR INIQUITIES AND DID NOT DESTROY
THEM. TIME AFTER MEIT HE RESTRAINED
HIS ANGER AND DID NOT STIR UP HIS FULL
TWHRA."

PSALM 78:38

1. _ _ _ _ _   _ _ _ _ _ _ _

2. _ _ _ _ _ _   _ _ _ _ _ _

3. _ _ _ _ _ _ _ _   _ _ _ _ _

    _ _ _ _ _ _

MULTIPLE CHOICE

ANGER IS JUST A FEELING, BUT IT IS WHAT YOU DO WITH IT THAT CAN MAKE IT RIGHT OR WRONG.

1. YOUR BROTHER CALLS YOU A NAME. WHAT SHOULD YOU DO?
   A) CALL HIM AN EVEN NASTIER NAME.
   B) TELL HIM THAT WASN'T NICE AND THAT YOU DIDN'T LIKE IT.
   C) IGNORE HIM AND DON'T SPEAK TO HIM AGAIN.

2. YOU WANT TO STAY OVERNIGHT AT A FRIEND'S HOUSE. YOUR PARENTS SAY NO.
   A) YOU SHOULD ARGUE WITH THEM.
   B) YOU SHOULD HAVE A TEMPER TANTRUM.
   C) YOU SHOULD ACCEPT THEIR ANSWER AND MAKE OTHER PLANS.

3. A FRIEND SHARES HER CANDY WITH EVERYONE ELSE, BUT LEAVES YOU OUT.
   A) CALL HER NAMES.
   B) TALK ABOUT HER BEHIND HER BACK.
   C) TELL HER PRIVATELY HOW YOU FEEL.

4. JUST BEFORE IT'S YOUR TURN IN THE HOT DOG LINE, SOMEONE BUTTS IN FRONT OF YOU.
- A) YELL AT THEM AND TELL THEM YOU'RE NEXT.
- B) POLITELY TELL THEM YOU ARE NEXT.
- C) PUSH THEM OUT OF THE WAY.

5. THE TEACHER EMBARRASSES YOU IN FRONT OF THE CLASS.
- A) TALK POLITELY WITH THE TEACHER AFTER CLASS.
- B) EMBARRASS THE TEACHER BACK.
- C) AFTER CLASS, PUT TACKS ON THE TEACHER'S CHAIR.

6. YOU SEE A GROUP OF KIDS PICKING ON YOUR FRIEND.
- A) RUN IN WITH FISTS FLYING.
- B) GO TO AN ADULT FOR HELP.
- C) GO STAND BESIDE YOUR FRIEND.

FILL THEM IN

ACTS OF THE SINFUL NATURE

LOOK UP GALATIANS 5:19-21 IN YOUR BIBLE.

ON THE NEXT PAGE, FILL IN THE BOXES WITH THE SINFUL ACTS.

SCRAMBLED VERSES

UNSCRAMBLE THE VERSES BELOW, THEN COMPLETE THE NEXT PAGE.

"NI UYRO GEANR OD TNO NSI: OD NTO TLE HET SNU OG WDNO HLIEW OYU EAR LTLIS AYGRN, DAN OD TON EIGV ETH LDVEI A HFTLOODO."

EPHESIANS 4:26-27

"TGE DRI FO LAL NSSETBTIRE, ERGA NDA GNARE, WGRBLAIN DAN AER-SNLD, NLAGO IWHT RYVEE MFRO FO MIALEC. EB IDKN DAN NAPIOOMTC-SAES OT EON HTRAENO, IIFVRGONG CHAE EOHRT, SJTU SA NI HTCIRS DGO GRFOEVA OYU."

EPHESIANS 4:31-32

FINISH *the* VERSE

USE THE CODE CHART BELOW TO FINISH THE
VERSE. (EG: K=24)

	1	2	3	4	5	6	7
1	A	B	C	D	E	F	G
2	H	I	J	K	L	M	N
3	O	P	Q	R	S	T	U
4	V	W	X	Y	Z		

"A ___ ___ ___ ___ GIVES ___ ___ ___ ___
16 31 31 25   16 37 25 25

___ ___ ___ ___ TO HIS ___ ___ ___ ___ ___,
41 15 27 36   11 27 17 15 34

BUT A ___ ___ ___ ___ ___ ___ ___
42 22 35 15   26 11 27

KEEPS ___ ___ ___ ___ ___ ___ ___
21 22 26 35 15 25 16

UNDER ___ ___ ___ ___ ___ ___ ___."
13 31 27 36 34 31 25

PROVERBS 29:11

29

FILL *in the* BLANKS

COMPASSION

SHOWING COMPASSION ISN'T JUST THE RIGHT THING TO DO...IT FEELS REAL GOOD TOO!

USING THE WORDS BELOW, COMPLETE THE VERSES ON THE NEXT PAGE.

COMPASSION
FORGAVE
GRIEVANCES
ANOTHER
HAVE
CLOTHE
HOLY
LORD

HUMILITY
CHOSEN
FORGIVE
GENTLENESS
BEAR
LOVED

"THEREFORE, AS GOD'S _____ PEOPLE, _____ AND DEARLY _____, _____ YOURSELVES WITH _____, KINDNESS, _____, _____ AND PATIENCE. _____WITH EACH OTHER AND _____ WHATEVER _____ YOU MAY _____ AGAINST ONE _____. FORGIVE AS THE _____ _____ YOU."

COLOSSIANS 3:12-13

SCRAMBLED VERSES

COMPASSION MEANS ACTION!

UNSCRAMBLE THE VERSES BELOW AND COMPLETE THE NEXT PAGE TO FIND SOME WAYS TO SHOW COMPASSION.

"ESBLS OESHT HOW CSPEEERTU YUO; LBSES NDA OD TNO RCSEU. EOEIRCJ IHWT HEOTS OWH JROIEEC; UMNOR THWI SOTHE OHW NRMUO. IVEL NI HYRNAOM HWIT NOE OAERNHT. OD OTN EB DORPU, UBT EB GLLIWIN OT TCSAOSEAI WHTI EOEPPL FO WLO TIIPSOON. OD TON EB CCTEINEOD."

32

"_____ _____ _____ _____   _____ _____ _____
_____ _____ _____   _____ _____ _____ _____
_____ _____ ;   _____ _____ _____ _____
_____ _____ _____   _____ _____ _____   _____ _____ .
_____ _____ _____   _____ _____ _____ _____
_____ _____ _____ _____ _____   _____ _____ _____   _____ _____ -
_____ _____ _____ _____ ;   _____ _____ _____
_____ _____ _____ _____   _____ _____ _____ _____
_____ _____ _____ _____ .   _____ _____ _____
_____ _____ _____ _____   _____ _____
_____ _____ _____   _____ _____ .
_____ _____ _____ _____   _____ _____ _____ _____ ,
_____ _____ _____ _____   _____ _____
_____ _____ _____ _____   _____ _____ _____ _____ .
_____ _____ _____ _____ _____   _____ _____ _____ _____ .
_____ _____ _____ _____ _____ _____   _____ _____   _____ _____ -
_____ _____ _____ _____ ."

ROMANS 12:14-16

WORD SEARCH

COMPASSION MEANS BEING CONCERNED FOR OTHERS

FIND THE WORDS UNDERLINED BELOW IN THE WORD SEARCH ON THE NEXT PAGE.

"DO NOTHING OUT OF <u>SELFISH</u> <u>AMBITION</u> OR VAIN <u>CONCEIT</u>, BUT IN <u>HUMILITY</u> CONSIDER OTHERS <u>BETTER</u> THAN YOURSELVES. EACH OF YOU <u>SHOULD</u> <u>LOOK</u> NOT ONLY TO YOUR OWN <u>INTERESTS</u>, BUT ALSO TO THE INTERESTS OF <u>OTHERS</u>."

PHILIPPIANS 2:3–4

```
K M W I B B C T I N B O
F B Y D B A Q N N Q S L
T C O N C E I T T U H W
O T H E R S T D E K O B
K K C P D V D T R E U L
H R Q O Y C L G E W L R
F J G O N T B X S R D D
G S J V B K F L T R T A
S D B E O L E S S I S M
P E T O R B V D H P T B
T P L H U M I L I T Y I
R Z T F B B D M S D N T
W A C T I N E S B F I I
H A P P B S D Z C H L O
Q L R V B P H K T K N N
```

FINISH *the* VERSE

USE THE CODE CHART BELOW TO FINISH THE
VERSES. (EG: K=24)

	1	2	3	4	5	6	7
1	A	B	C	D	E	F	G
2	H	I	J	K	L	M	N
3	O	P	Q	R	S	T	U
4	V	W	X	Y	Z		

"___ ___ ___ ___ ___ ___ ___ ___ , IF
  12 34 31 36 21 15 34 35

___ ___ ___ ___ ___ ___ ___ IS
 35 31 26 15 31 27 15

___ ___ ___ ___ ___ ___ IN A ___ ___ , YOU
 13 11 37 17 21 36   35 22 27

WHO ARE ___ ___ ___ ___ ___ ___ ___ ___ ___
         35 32 22 34 22 36 37 11 25

___ ___ ___ ___ ___ ___ ___ ___ ___ ___ ___ ___ ___
 35 21 31 37 25 14   34 15 35 36 31 34 15

HIM ___ ___ ___ ___ ___ ___ . BUT
    17 15 27 36 25 44

___ ___ ___ ___ ___ YOURSELF, OR YOU
 42 11 36 13 21

___ ___ ___ ___ MAY BE ___ ___ ___ ___ ___ ___ .
 11 25 35 31   36 15 26 32 36 15 14

___ ___ ___ ___ ___ ___ ___ ___ OTHER'S
 13 11 34 34 44 15 11 13 21

___ ___ ___ ___ ___ ___ ___ , AND IN ___ ___ ___ ___
 12 37 34 14 15 27 36   36 21 22 35

WAY YOU WILL ___ ___ ___ ___ ___ ___ ___
        16 37 25 16 22 25 25

THE ___ ___ ___ OF ___ ___ ___ ___ ___ ___ ."
   25 11 42   13 21 34 22 35 36

GALATIANS 6:1-2

DOUBLE *the* FUN

UNSCRAMBLE THE UNDERLINED WORDS IN EACH VERSE. ON THE NEXT PAGE, PLACE YOUR ANSWERS IN THE SPACES PROVIDED AND THEN COMPLETE THE CROSSWORD PUZZLE.

1. "HAVE <u>ECMYR</u> ON ME, O GOD, ACCORDING TO YOUR UNFAILING <u>OELV</u>; ACCORDING TO YOUR GREAT COMPASSION BLOT OUT MY TRANSGRESSIONS."

   PSALM 51:1

2. "THE LORD IS <u>UCGRISAO</u> AND <u>GESOIHUTR</u>; OUR GOD IS FULL OF COMPASSION."

   PSALM 116:5

3. "THE <u>DOLR</u> IS GOOD TO ALL; HE HAS <u>OSOIPMCSAN</u> ON ALL HE HAS MADE."

   PSALM 145:9

1. _ _ _ _ _ _   _ _ _ _

2. _ _ _ _ _ _ _ _ _ _ _ _ _

   _ _ _ _ _ _ _ _ _ _ _ _

3. _ _ _ _

   _ _ _ _ _ _ _ _ _ _ _ _

SECRET CODES

LOVE ONE ANOTHER

TO SOLVE THE CODED VERSES BELOW, LOOK AT EACH LETTER AND WRITE THE ONE THAT COMES BEFORE IT IN THE ALPHABET.

"BCPWF BMM, MPWF FBDI PUIFS EFFQMZ, CFDBVTF MPWF DPWFST PWFS B NVMUJUVEF PG TJOT. PGGFS IPTQJUBMJUZ UP POF BOPUIFS XJUIPVU HSVNCMJOH."

A B C D E F G H I J K L M N O P Q R S T
U V W X Y Z

"_ _ _ _ _ _   _ _ _ _, _ _ _ _ _

_ _ _ _ _ _   _ _ _ _ _

_ _ _ _ _ _ _ _,   _ _ -

_ _ _ _ _ _ _   _ _ _ _

_ _ _ _ _ _ _   _ _ _ _

_ _ _ _ _ _ _ _ _ _

_ _ _ _ _ _.   _ _ _ _ _

_ _ _ _ _ _ _ _ _ _ _

_ _ _ _ _ _ _ _ _ _

_ _ _ _ _ _ _ _   _ _ _ _ _ -

_ _ _ _ _."

1 PETER 4:8-9

41

FILL *in the* BLANKS

A SPECIAL PROMISE

SOMETIMES, IT CAN BE HARD TO BE COMPAS-SIONATE, BUT DOING SO WILL HELP YOU TO DO THE RIGHT THING IN EVERY SITUATION.

USING THE WORDS BELOW, COMPLETE THE VERSES ON THE NEXT PAGE.

INSULT	FINALLY
SYMPATHETIC	BLESSING
LIVE	HUMBLE
EVIL	CALLED
BROTHERS	COMPASSIONATE
HARMONY	REPAY
INHERIT	BLESSING

"_____, ALL OF YOU, _____
IN _____ WITH ONE
ANOTHER; BE _____, LOVE
AS _____, BE _____
AND _____. DO NOT _____
EVIL WITH _____ OR INSULT WITH
_____, BUT WITH _____,
BECAUSE TO THIS YOU WERE _____
SO THAT YOU MAY _____ A
_____."

1 PETER 3:8-9

FINISH *the* VERSE

HATRED

HAVE YOU EVER BEEN TOLD THAT IT'S WRONG TO HATE? BUT...SOMETIMES, YOU DO FEEL IT.

COULD THERE EVER BE A TIME THAT IT IS OKAY TO HATE? IS THERE ANYTHING THAT GOD HATES? LET'S FIND OUT!

USE THE CODE CHART BELOW TO FINISH THE VERSES. (EG: K=24)

	1	2	3	4	5	6	7
1	A	B	C	D	E	F	G
2	H	I	J	K	L	M	N
3	O	P	Q	R	S	T	U
4	V	W	X	Y	Z		

"THERE ARE ___ ___ ___ THINGS THE
       35 22 43

___ ___ ___ ___   ___ ___ ___ ___ ___,
25 31 34 14   21 11 36 15 35

___ ___ ___ ___ ___   THAT   ARE
35 15 41 15 27

                                      TO
___ ___ ___ ___ ___ ___ ___ ___ ___ ___
14 15 36 15 35 36   11 12 25 15

HIM: HAUGHTY ___ ___ ___ ___, A
                15 44 15 35

___ ___ ___ ___ ___ TONGUE,   ___ ___ ___ ___ ___
25 44 22 27 17   21 11 27 14 35

THAT SHED ___ ___ ___ ___ ___ ___ ___ ___
           22 27 27 31 13 15 27 36

BLOOD, A   HEART   THAT
                                  WICKED
___ ___ ___ ___ ___ ___ ___
14 15 41 22 35 15 35

___ ___ ___ ___ ___ ___ ___, ___ ___ ___ ___
35 13 21 15 26 15 35   16 15 15 36

THAT ARE ___ ___ ___ ___ ___ ___ TO RUSH
          33 37 22 13 24

INTO ___ ___ ___ ___, A FALSE WITNESS
      15 41 22 25

WHO ___ ___ ___ ___ ___ OUT LIES AND A
     32 31 37 34 35

___ ___ ___ WHO STIRS UP ___ ___ ___ -
26 11 27   14 22 35

___ ___ ___ ___ ___ ___ ___ AMONG
35 15 27 35 22 31 27

___ ___ ___ ___ ___ ___ ___ ___."
12 34 31 36 21 15 34 35

PROVERBS 6:16-19

45

SCRAMBLED VERSES

WHAT DOES GOD SAY?

IF IT'S OKAY FOR GOD TO HATE CERTAIN THINGS, IS THERE EVER A TIME THAT IT'S ALL RIGHT FOR ME TO HATE SOMETHING?

UNSCRAMBLE THE VERSES BELOW AND COMPLETE THE NEXT PAGE.

"UYO ERA TNO A DGO OHW STKAE EPRLUEAS NI VIEL; HTWI UOY HET DWCKIE TNNAOC DLWLE. ETH TRRONGAA TNCONA DSTAN NI RYOU ECPRNESE; UYO ETHA LAL WOH OD GNWOR."

46

"—— — — —— — —— — —

—— — — —— — —— — —

—— — — —— — —— — —— —

—— — —; —— — —— —

—— — —— —— — —— -

—— — —— —— —. —— —

—— —— —— —— — —— -

—— — —— — —— — ——

—— — —— —— —— —;

—— — —— — —— — —— —

—— — —— — —— —— —."

SCRAMBLED VERSES

A TIME FOR EVERYTHING

LET'S DIG DEEPER AND FIND OUT FROM GOD'S WORD WHEN THERE MAY BE A TIME TO HATE.

LOOK UP THE VERSES BELOW AND PUT THE WORDS IN THEIR PROPER ORDER.

IN ECCLESIASTES 3:1, IT SAYS:

EVERYTHING, TIME HEAVEN." "THERE A UNDER IS ACTIVITY FOR EVERY A FOR SEASON AND

AND IN VERSE 3:8, IT SAYS:

TIME "A LOVE TIME HATE." TO AND A TO

"_____ _____ ____ ____

_____ _____,

_____ ____ _____ _____

_____ _____

_____ _____."

ECCLESIASTES 3:1

"_ _____ _____ _____

_____ ____ _____ _____

_____."

ECCLESIASTES 3:8

49

CROSSWORD

DIG, DIG, DIG!

ACROSS

1. "I GAIN UNDERSTANDING FROM YOUR
   _____."

2. "THEREFORE I _____ EVERY WRONG
   PATH."   PSALM 119:104

3. "I HATE _____-MINDED MEN."

4. "BUT I _____ YOUR LAW."
                                             PSALM 119:113

DOWN

1. "YOU ARE MY REFUGE AND MY _____."

2. "I HAVE PUT MY _____ IN YOUR
   WORD."

3. "AWAY FROM ME, YOU EVIL-_____."

4. "THAT I MAY KEEP THE COMMANDS OF
   MY _____."
                                             PSALM 119:114-115

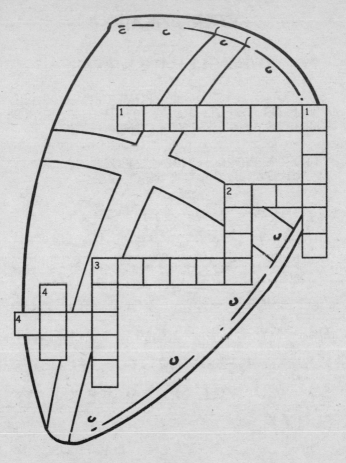

51

WORD SEARCH

WHEN IS HATE WRONG?

SOMEONE HAS DONE SOMETHING REALLY MEAN OR AWFUL. DO YOU HATE THE PERSON OR HATE WHAT THEY'VE DONE?

FIND THE WORDS UNDERLINED BELOW IN THE WORD SEARCH ON THE NEXT PAGE.

"DO NOT <u>HATE</u> YOUR <u>BROTHER</u> IN YOUR <u>HEART</u>. <u>REBUKE</u> YOUR <u>NEIGHBOR</u> <u>FRANKLY</u> SO YOU WILL NOT <u>SHARE</u> IN HIS <u>GUILT</u>."

LEVITICUS 19:17

52

```
E W D P L S K F M D P B
F H J R O N L Q S K T L
Z K L J R E B U K E D R
K M Y G F I J I K B F D
F B T H T G L D R C H X
T R H D P H B N N T K M
B T A N V B R O T H E R
K K Q N B O B D L Q S I
H R G P K R N T R D N G
E H J Z C L S G F K I U
T S E J R D Y K S P E I
A D T A D S C L T R N L
H C L T R V Q S A R O T
T P T C N T I H H R L Z
R Z C V B T S L G I W J
```

FILL *in the* BLANKS

GOD'S WORD IS CLEAR!

IT'S OKAY TO SOMETIMES HATE CERTAIN THINGS THAT OTHERS MAY DO, BUT IT IS WRONG TO HATE THE PERSON.

USING THE WORDS BELOW, COMPLETE THE VERSES ON THE NEXT PAGE.

TELL
CURSE
PRAY
LOVE
MISTREAT
HATE
GOOD
ENEMIES
BLESS
HEAR

"BUT I _____ YOU WHO _____

ME: _____ YOUR _____,

DO _____ TO THOSE WHO _____

YOU, _____ THOSE WHO _____

YOU, _____ FOR THOSE WHO

_____ YOU."

LUKE 6:27-28

FINISH *the* VERSE

L♥VE
A FEELING...OR AN ACTION?

IF LOVE IS JUST A FEELING, WHAT HAPPENS WHEN WE GET ANGRY WITH SOMEONE? DO WE NO LONGER LOVE THEM?

WHAT IF OUR PARENTS WANT US TO DO SOMETHING WE JUST DON'T WANT TO DO; WE COULD BE REALLY ANGRY AT THEM. BECAUSE WE DON'T HAVE LOVING FEELINGS RIGHT AT THAT MOMENT, DOES THAT MEAN WE NO LONGER LOVE THEM?

USE THE CODE CHART BELOW TO FINISH THE VERSE. (EG: K=24)

	1	2	3	4	5	6	7
1	A	B	C	D	E	F	G
2	H	I	J	K	L	M	N
3	O	P	Q	R	S	T	U
4	V	W	X	Y	Z		

HOW DOES GOD LOVE US?

"FOR __ __ __ SO __ __ __ __ __
17 31 14   25 31 41 15 14

THE __ __ __ __ __ THAT HE
42 31 34 25 14

__ __ __ __ __ __ __ __ __ __
17 11 41 15 21 22 35 31 27 15

AND __ __ __ __ __ __ __, THAT
31 27 25 44 35 31 27

BELIEVES __ __
42 21 31 15 41 15 34   22 27

NOT
__ __ __ __ __ __ __
21 22 26 35 21 11 25 25

BUT HAVE
__ __ __ __ __ __
32 15 34 22 35 21

__ __ __ __ __ __ __ __ __ __ __."
15 36 15 34 27 11 25 25 22 16 15

JOHN 3:16

MAYBE, IF WE CHOOSE TO TREAT OTHERS KINDLY,
NO MATTER WHAT, OR WE DO AS ASKED, OUR *ACT*
OF OBEDIANCE DEMONSTRATES OUR LOVE!

COLOR *the* PICTURE

LOVE IN ACTION!

IN 1 JOHN 3:16 AND 18 THE APOSTLE JOHN TELLS US OF THE KIND OF LOVE THAT GOD HAS FOR US AND HOW WE SHOULD ACT BECAUSE OF THAT LOVE.

"THIS IS HOW WE KNOW WHAT LOVE IS: JESUS CHRIST LAID DOWN HIS LIFE FOR US."

and:

"DEAR CHILDREN, LET US NOT LOVE WITH WORDS OR TONGUE BUT WITH ACTIONS AND IN TRUTH."

SECRET CODES

LOVE ONE ANOTHER

TO SOLVE THE CODED VERSES BELOW, LOOK AT EACH LETTER AND WRITE THE ONE THAT COMES BEFORE IT IN THE ALPHABET.

"B OFX DPNNBOE J HJWF ZPV: MPWF POF BOPUIFS. BT J IBWF MPWFE ZPV, TP ZPV NVTU MPWF POF BOPUIFS. CZ UIJT BMM NFO XJMM LOPX UIBU ZPV BSF NZ EJTDJQMFT, JG ZPV MPWF POF BOPUIFS."

A B C D E F G H I J K L M N O P Q R S T
U V W X Y Z

"__ ___ ___ ___ ___ ___

__ ___ ___ ___ ___:

__ __ __ __ __ __

__ __ __ __ __ __ .

__ __ __ __ __ __

__ __ __ ___ , __ __ __ __

__ __ __ __ __ __ __

__ __ __ __ __ __ . __ ___

__ __ __ __ ___ __

__ __ __ ___ __ __ ___

__ ___ __ __ __ ___

__ __ __ __ , __ __ __ __

__ __ __ __ __ ___ -

___ __ __ ."

JOHN 13:34-35

MULTIPLE CHOICE

"YOU HAVE HEARD THAT IT WAS SAID, 'LOVE YOUR NEIGHBOR AND HATE YOUR ENEMY.' BUT I TELL YOU: LOVE YOUR ENEMIES AND PRAY FOR THOSE WHO PERSECUTE YOU."

MATTHEW 5:43-44

BASED ON THE VERSES ABOVE, WHAT SHOULD BE DONE IN THE FOLLOWING SITUATIONS?

1. A GIRL AT SCHOOL HAS BEEN SPREADING LIES ABOUT YOU.
   - A) CHALLENGE HER TO A FIGHT.
   - B) INVITE HER TO YOUR HOUSE AND GET TO KNOW HER.
   - C) REPORT HER TO THE PRINCIPAL.

2. SOMEONE STOLE YOUR BIKE AND YOU KNOW WHO IT IS.
   - A) PHONE THE POLICE.
   - B) ASK FOR IT BACK AND OFFER YOUR OLD BIKE FOR FREE.
   - C) YOU AND YOUR BUDDIES SHOULD GO AND CONFRONT HIM.

3. SOMEONE YOU THOUGHT WAS YOUR
   FRIEND COPIED YOUR BOOK REPORT AND
   HAS BLAMED YOU FOR CHEATING.
   - A) GOD REVEALS THE TRUTH AND YOU
     DECIDE YOU CAN NO LONGER BE
     FRIENDS.
   - B) YOU TAKE THE BLAME.
   - C) GOD REVEALS THE TRUTH AND YOU
     OFFER FORGIVENESS.

4. KIDS AT SCHOOL LAUGH AT YOU BECAUSE
   OF YOUR FAITH.
   - A) IN THE FUTURE, YOU DECIDE TO
     KEEP YOUR FAITH A SECRET.
   - B) YOU DECIDE TO USE THIS AS AN
     OPPORTUNITY TO SHARE YOUR
     FAITH.
   - C) BOLDLY CONFRONT THEM AND
     CONDEMN THEM FOR THEIR SIN.

5. JESUS WAS UNFAIRLY JUDGED AND SENT
   TO THE CROSS.
   - A) HE ASKED HIS FATHER TO FORGIVE
     THOSE RESPONSIBLE, THEN DIED
     FOR US ALL.
   - B) HE CALLED UPON LEGIONS OF
     ANGELS TO SAVE HIM.
   - C) HE CRIED OUT FOR MERCY.

DOUBLE *the* FUN

UNSCRAMBLE THE UNDERLINED WORDS IN EACH VERSE. ON THE NEXT PAGE, PLACE YOUR ANSWERS IN THE SPACES PROVIDED AND THEN COMPLETE THE CROSSWORD PUZZLE.

1. "I LOVE YOU, O LORD, MY <u>RGSTTHNE</u>."

   PSALM 18:1

2. "SURELY <u>ODSOGESN</u> AND <u>VEOL</u> WILL FOL-
   LOW ME ALL THE DAYS OF MY <u>FLEI</u>, AND
   I WILL <u>ELWDL</u> IN THE <u>OHESU</u> OF THE
   LORD FOREVER."

   PSALM 23:6

3. "MAY YOUR UNFAILING LOVE <u>TRSE</u> UPON
   US, O LORD, EVEN AS WE PUT OUR <u>OPHE</u>
   IN YOU."

   PSALM 33:22

1. ___ ___ ___ ___ ___ ___ ___

2. ___ ___ ___ ___ ___ ___ ___ ___ ___ ___

   ___ ___ ___ ___ ___ ___

   ___ ___ ___ ___

3. ___ ___ ___ ___ ___ ___ ___

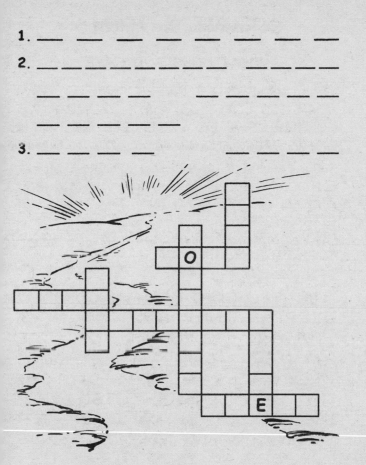

SCRAMBLED VERSES

WHAT DOES GOD SAY?

WHEN WE BEGIN TO UNDERSTAND JUST HOW MUCH GOD LOVES US, AND HOW MUCH WE DON'T DESERVE IT, WE REALIZE THE DEPTH OF HIS MERCY AND GRACE.

THIS CAN HELP US TO SEE OTHERS DIFFER-ENTLY AND HOPEFULLY OFFER THEM GRACE AS WELL IF THEY DO THINGS THAT HURT US.

UNSCRAMBLE THE VERSE BELOW AND COMPLETE THE NEXT PAGE.

"TBU VLEO URYO MEEIENS, OD ODGO OT ETMH, NDA NLDE OT MEHT TTUIWHO PICXEETGN OT TGE HAYNTGIN CAKB. TNEH UORY WREADR LILW EB TGERA, DAN OYU IWLL EB ONSS FO HET OTSM GIHH, SBCEEUA EH SI DKNI OT TEH TGUULERFAN DNA WDKEIC."

"____ ____ ____
_____, ____ ____ ____
__ __ ____ __, ____
____ ____ ____ ____
____ ____ ____ __-
____ ____ ____ ____
_____ ____.
__ ____ ____ __-
__ ____ ____ __
____, ____ __ ____
__ ____ ____ ____
____ ____ ____,
____ ____ ____ ____
____ __ __ ____
__ __ ____ ____
___ ____ ___."

LUKE 6:35

67

CROSSWORD

A FRAGRANT OFFERING

ACROSS

1. "BE _____ OF GOD, THEREFORE."
2. "AS DEARLY LOVED _____."
3. "_____ LIVE A LIFE OF LOVE."
4. "JUST AS _____ LOVED US."

DOWN

1. "AND GAVE _____ UP FOR US."
2. "AS A _____ OFFERING."
3. "AND _____ TO GOD."

EPHESIANS 5:1-2

68

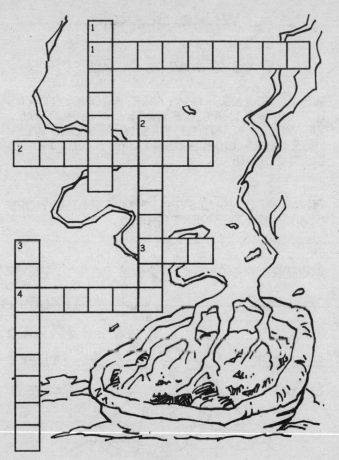

WORD SEARCH

LOVE COVERS IT ALL!

WE DO THINGS THAT ARE WRONG...OTHERS DO THINGS THAT ARE WRONG AND HURTFUL. WE WOULD WANT OTHERS TO RESPOND WITH LOVE AND FORGIVE US; PERHAPS WE SHOULD DO THE SAME?

FIND THE SINS, LISTED BELOW, IN THE WORD SEARCH ON THE NEXT PAGE.

ANGER	ENVY
JEALOUSY	STEALING
GOSSIP	HATRED
SLANDER	THEFT
LYING	CHEATING

```
T H J G F G L D R D K R
F E N V Y H B N E H S G
A M Y D P J R R T Q N C
K N T N V E T D L D P F
F R G N B A N T R K T L
T T Q E H L S G F P H T
B K G Z R O Y K S R E Z
K R J J R U C L T R F J
H H T A D S Q S D R T R
M S L T L Y I N G I B E
C H E A T I N G O P L D
H C C V B K F M S T R N
T P P L S L Q S S D D A
S T E A L I N G I F X L
W D J R B J I K P H M S
```

MULTIPLE CHOICE

"DO TO OTHERS AS YOU WOULD HAVE THEM
DO TO YOU."

LUKE 6:31

AFTER READING THE VERSE ABOVE, WHAT WOULD
BE THE RIGHT CHOICES BELOW?

1. PETER BETRAYED JESUS THE NIGHT OF HIS
   TRIAL.
   - A) JESUS FOREVER BANNED HIM FROM
     HEAVEN.
   - B) JESUS EXPECTED PETER TO MAKE IT
     UP TO HIM.
   - C) JESUS FORGAVE HIM.

2. JESUS TOLD OF A MAN WHO WAS FORGIVEN
   HIS DEBTS.
   - A) THE MAN WAS NOW FREE TO COLLECT
     FROM THOSE WHO OWED HIM.
   - B) HE SHOULD FORGIVE OTHERS THEIR
     DEBTS TO HIM.
   - C) HE SHOULD PAY IT BACK ANYWAY.

3. BOTH YOU AND YOUR FRIEND HAVE BEEN
   OFFERED THE SAME ROLE IN THE SCHOOL
   PLAY.
   - A) DO YOUR BEST AT THE AUDITION.
   - B) OFFER A BRIBE TO GET THE PART.
   - C) DECLINE THE PART.

4. JESUS TOLD OF A FATHER WHO WAITED
   FOR A REBELLIOUS SON TO RETURN HOME.
   - A) THE FATHER SHOULD WELCOME HIM
     BACK AND CELEBRATE.
   - B) HE SHOULD NOT ALLOW THE SON
     BACK UNTIL HE PAYS BACK THE
     MONEY HE SQUANDERED.
   - C) HE SHOULD TAKE HIM BACK BUT
     TREAT HIM AS ONE OF HIS
     SERVANTS.

5. AN INJURED MAN LIES ON THE SIDE OF
   THE ROAD.
   - A) PASS BY, HOPING SOMEONE ELSE
     WILL TAKE CARE OF HIM.
   - B) MAKE HIM COMFORTABLE, THEN
     RUN FOR HELP.
   - C) CHECK HIS CLOTHING FOR ANY
     VALUABLES.

6. YOUR PARENTS HAVE ASKED A FAVOR, THAT
   YOU WOULD CLEAN THE CARS.
   - A) YOU AGREE BUT DECIDE LATER NOT
     TO BOTHER.
   - B) YOU WILL...AS LONG AS THEY PAY
     YOU.
   - C) YOU DO IT WILLINGLY, REALIZING
     HOW MUCH THEY DO FOR YOU.

FINISH *the* VERSE

USE THE CODE CHART BELOW TO FINISH THE VERSES. (EG: K=24)

	1	2	3	4	5	6	7
1	A	B	C	D	E	F	G
2	H	I	J	K	L	M	N
3	O	P	Q	R	S	T	U
4	V	W	X	Y	Z		

"IF YOU __ __ __ __ THOSE WHO
     25 31 41 15

__ __ __ __ YOU, WHAT __ __ __ __ __ __
25 31 41 15   13 34 15 14 22 36

IS __ __ __ __ TO YOU? EVEN
   36 21 11 36

' __ __ __ __ __ __ __ ' __ __ __ __
35 22 27 27 15 34 35   25 31 41 15

__ __ __ __ __ WHO __ __ __ __
36 21 31 35 15   25 31 41 15

THEM. AND IF YOU DO __ __ __ __TO
            17 31 31 14

__ __ __ __ __ WHO ARE __ __ __ __
36 21 31 35 15   17 31 31 14

TO YOU, WHAT __ __ __ __ __ __ IS
         13 34 15 14 22 36

THAT TO __ __ __? EVEN
         44 31 37

' __ __ __ __ __ __ __ ' DO THAT.
35 22 27 27 15 34 35

LUKE 6:32-33

SCRAMBLED VERSES

GOD'S WAY IS CERTAINLY DIFFERENT!

THE WORLD WOULD LEAD YOU TO BELIEVE THAT YOU SHOULD PUT YOURSELF ABOVE ALL OTHERS. BUT YOU'VE LEARNED HOW GOD WANTS YOU TO THINK, THAT THERE IS GREAT BLESSING IN PUTTING OTHERS BEFORE YOURSELF.

TRY IT HIS WAY!

LOOK UP THE VERSES BELOW AND PUT THE WORDS IN THEIR PROPER ORDER.

IN PROVERBS 24:17, IT SAYS:

ENEMY GLOAT WHEN NOT REJOICE," YOUR STUMBLES, "DO HEART FALLS; YOUR NOT LET HE DO WHEN

AND IN ROMANS 12:14, IT SAYS:

YOU; THOSE CURSE." PERSECUTE "BLESS NOT WHO AND BLESS DO

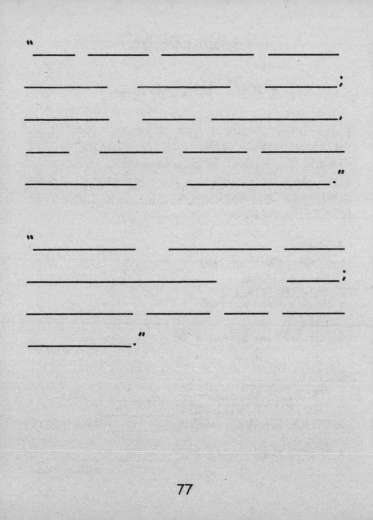

CROSSWORD

FEAR WORRY

FEAR AND WORRY! THESE TWO ARE REAL FAITH-BUSTERS AND ARE GUARANTEED TO KNOCK YOU RIGHT OFF YOUR FEET.

BUT, *HOW* CAN YOU OVERCOME THEM? LET'S CONTINUE ON AND YOU'LL SEE HOW OVER THE NEXT FEW PAGES.

ACROSS

1. "THE LORD IS MY _____ AND MY SALVATION."
2. "WHOM SHALL I _____?"
3. "THE LORD IS THE _____ OF MY LIFE."
4. "OF WHOM SHALL I BE _____?"

PSALM 27:1

DOWN

1. "THOUGH AN ARMY _____ ME."
2. "MY HEART WILL NOT _____."
3. "THOUGH WAR BREAK _____ AGAINST ME."
4. "EVEN THEN WILL I BE _____."

PSALM 27:3

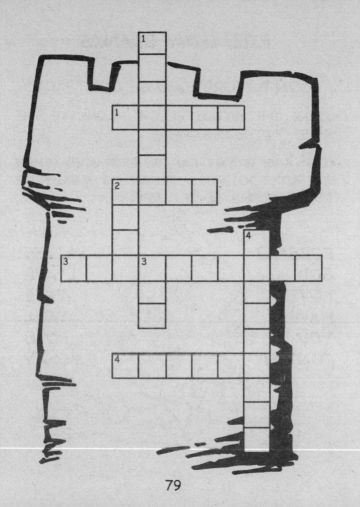

FILL *in the* BLANKS

DON'T WORRY *and* BE CONTENT!

USING THE WORDS BELOW, COMPLETE THE VERSE ON THE NEXT PAGE.

FEAR AND WORRY CAN BE PRODUCED WHEN WE PUT TOO MUCH TRUST IN MONEY OR POSSESSIONS. SO BE CAREFUL.

FORSAKE   LIVES
GOD   LEAVE
NEVER   FREE
HAVE   WILL
YOU   LOVE
CONTENT   MONEY

"KEEP YOUR _____ _____

FROM THE _____ OF _____

AND BE _____ WITH

WHAT YOU _____, BECAUSE

_____ HAS SAID, '_____ WILL

I _____ _____; NEVER _____

I _____ YOU.'"

HEBREWS 13:5

81

SECRET CODES

PUT YOUR TRUST IN THE LORD

TO SOLVE THE CODED VERSES BELOW, LOOK AT EACH LETTER AND WRITE THE ONE THAT COMES BEFORE IT IN THE ALPHABET.

"DBTU ZPVS DBSFT PO UIF MPSE BOE
IF XJMM TVTUBJO ZPV; IF XJMM
OFWFS MFU UIF SJHIUFPVT GBMM."

PSALM 55:22

"CVU ZPV, P HPE, XJMM CSJOH EPXO
UIF XJDLFE JOUP UIF QJU PG
DPSSVQUJPO; CMPPEUIJSTUZ BOE
EFDFJUGVM NFO XJMM OPU MJWF
PVU IBMG UIFJS EBZT. CVU BT GPS
NF, J USVTU JO ZPV."

PSALM 55:23

A B C D E F G H I J K L M N O P Q R S T
U V W X Y Z

DOUBLE *the* FUN

UNSCRAMBLE THE UNDERLINED WORDS IN
EACH VERSE. ON THE NEXT PAGE, PLACE YOUR
ANSWERS IN THE SPACES PROVIDED AND
THEN COMPLETE THE CROSSWORD PUZZLE.

1. "THE <u>ARFE</u> OF THE LORD IS <u>UPER</u>,
ENDURING <u>RREEFVO</u>. THE <u>AEONNRICSD</u>
OF THE LORD ARE SURE AND ALTOGETHER
RIGHTEOUS."

PSALM 19:9

2. "EVEN THOUGH I <u>KAWL</u> THROUGH THE
<u>YALVLE</u> OF THE <u>HAWSOD</u> OF DEATH,
I WILL FEAR NO <u>LEIV</u>, FOR YOU ARE
WITH ME; YOUR <u>DRO</u> AND YOUR
STAFF, THEY <u>OFMTCOR</u> ME."

PSALM 23:4

1. __ __ __ __ __   __ __ __ __

__ __ __ __ __ __

__ __ __ __ __ __ __

2. __ __ __ __   __ __ __ __ __

__ __ __ __   __ __ __

__ __ __   __ __ __ __ __

85

SCRAMBLED VERSES

HOW VALUABLE ARE YOU?

TO FIND OUT, LOOK UP THE VERSES BELOW
AND PUT THE WORDS IN THEIR PROPER
ORDER.

 IN MATTHEW 6:25-26, IT SAYS:

WORRY YOU IMPORTANT "THEREFORE NOT
FOOD, MORE WHAT IMPORTANT I YOU,
CLOTHES?" DRINK; ABOUT BODY EAT MORE
THE LIFE, YOUR TELL WILL WHAT DO
YOUR WEAR. BODY, YOU LIFE AND ABOUT
OR THAN IS WILL OR THAN NOT

BIRDS FATHER MUCH THEM. HEAVENLY DO
VALUABLE "LOOK THAN AIR; REAP STORE
MORE SOW BARNS, AWAY AT THE YOUR OF
FEEDS NOT OR NOT THEY OR IN THE
THEY?" AND YOU YET ARE

FINISH the VERSE

USE THE CODE CHART BELOW TO FINISH THE VERSES. (EG: K=24)

	1	2	3	4	5	6	7
1	A	B	C	D	E	F	G
2	H	I	J	K	L	M	N
3	O	P	Q	R	S	T	U
4	V	W	X	Y	Z		

88

"___ ___ ___ OF ___ ___ ___ BY
  42 21 31   44 31 37

CAN ADD A

___ ___ ___ ___ ___ ___ ___ ___
42 31 34 34 44 22 27 17

___ ___ ___ ___ ___ ___ ___ ___ ___ TO
35 22 27 17 25 15   21 31 37 34

HIS ___ ___ ___ ___? AND ___ ___ ___ DO
    25 22 16 15   42 21 44

YOU WORRY ___ ___ ___ ___ ___
                 11 12 31 37 36

___ ___ ___ ___ ___ ___ ___? SEE HOW THE
13 25 31 36 21 15 35

___ ___ ___ ___ ___ ___ OF THE
25 22 25 22 15 35

THEY

___ ___ ___ ___ ___ ___ ___ ___ ___. THEY
16 22 15 25 14   17 34 31 42

DO NOT ___ ___ ___ ___ ___ OR
          25 11 12 31 34

___ ___ ___ ___."
35 32 22 27

MATTHEW 6:27-28

89

WORD SEARCH

FIND THE WORDS UNDERLINED BELOW IN THE WORD SEARCH ON THE NEXT PAGE.

"YET I <u>TELL</u> YOU THAT NOT EVEN <u>SOLOMON</u> IN ALL HIS <u>SPLENDOR</u> WAS <u>DRESSED</u> LIKE ONE OF THESE. IF THAT IS HOW GOD <u>CLOTHES</u> THE <u>GRASS</u> OF THE <u>FIELD</u>, WHICH IS HERE <u>TODAY</u> AND <u>TOMORROW</u> IS <u>THROWN</u> INTO THE <u>FIRE</u>, WILL HE NOT MUCH MORE <u>CLOTHE</u> YOU, O YOU OF LITTLE <u>FAITH</u>?"

MATTHEW 6:29-30

```
F H T D F Q B F K D D L
C L O T H E S Q K T F V
D R D N P G L T E E T K
E T A P V F B R N L O Q
S A Y Z X B I H T L M X
S R I J B F B E C Q O M
E H T T K R M T L D R C
R S O L O M O N L D R L
D D P G R D N K R P O G
N C Z L D S S L F R W B
B W P C E S Y F S B N H
H Z O V A N C H A R X L
T D J R B T D L Z I L T
R J G Z H K D O H P T Z
W T C L O T H E R T B H
```

SECRET CODES

SO...DON'T WORRY!

TO SOLVE THE CODED VERSES BELOW, LOOK AT EACH LETTER AND WRITE THE ONE THAT COMES BEFORE IT IN THE ALPHABET.

"TP EP OPU XPSSZ, TBZJOH, 'XIBU TIBMM XF FBU?' PS 'ZIBU TIBMM XF ESJOL?' PS 'XIBU TIBMM XF XFBS?'"

MATTHEW 6:31

"EP OPU CF BOYJPVT BCPVU BOZUIJOH, CVU JO FWFSZUIJOH, CZ QSBZFS BOE QFUJUJPO, XJUI UIBOLTHJWJOH, QSFTFOU ZPVS SFRVFTUT UP HPE."

PHILIPPIANS 4:6

ABCDEFGHIJKLMNOPQRST
UVWXYZ

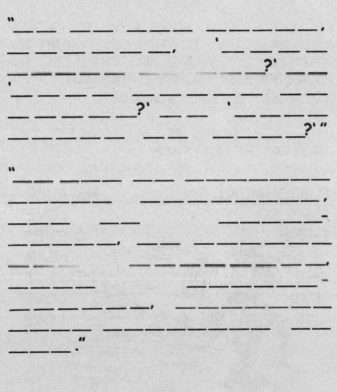

FILL *in the* BLANKS

NO NEED TO FEAR, NO NEED TO WORRY!

AS YOU'VE SEEN, GOD'S LOVE IS PRETTY AWESOME. TRUST IN THAT LOVE, TRUST IN WHAT GOD IS WILLING AND ABLE TO DO IN YOUR LIFE AND YOU WILL FIND THAT FEAR AND WORRY WILL BE OVERCOME!

USING THE WORDS BELOW, COMPLETE THE VERSE ON THE NEXT PAGE.

PUNISHMENT   BECAUSE
PERFECT   LOVE
THERE   DRIVES
FEARS   FEAR
ONE   PERFECT
FEAR   LOVE
NOT   LOVE

94

"_____ IS NO _____ IN

_____. BUT _____

_____ _____ OUT FEAR,

_____ _____ HAS TO

DO WITH _____.

THE _____ WHO _____ IS

_____ MADE _____ IN

_____."   1 JOHN 4:18

CROSSWORD

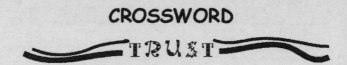

TRUST

YOU'VE LEARNED ABOUT THE MOST IMPORTANT THING OF ALL...GOD'S LOVE FOR YOU. YOU'VE LEARNED HOW TO OVERCOME FEELINGS THAT CAN HARM YOU OR OTHERS AND HOW THAT INVOLVES TRUSTING GOD.

LET'S DISCOVER MORE ABOUT TRUST!

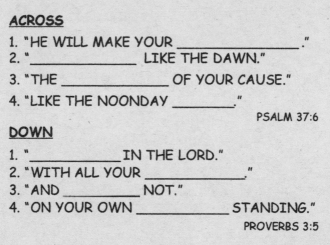

ACROSS

1. "HE WILL MAKE YOUR _____."
2. "_____ LIKE THE DAWN."
3. "THE _____ OF YOUR CAUSE."
4. "LIKE THE NOONDAY _____."

PSALM 37:6

DOWN

1. "_____ IN THE LORD."
2. "WITH ALL YOUR _____."
3. "AND _____ NOT."
4. "ON YOUR OWN _____ STANDING."

PROVERBS 3:5

96

97

FINISH *the* VERSE

TRUST AND REJOICE!

YOU CAN KNOW AN INCREDIBLE JOY WHEN
YOU PUT YOUR TRUST IN THE LORD. BECAUSE
YOU KNOW HOW MUCH HE LOVES YOU, YOU
CAN BELIEVE THAT HE WILL ALWAYS WORK
OUT EVERYTHING FOR THE BEST.

USE THE CODE CHART BELOW TO FINISH THE
VERSE. (EG: K=24)

	1	2	3	4	5	6	7
1	A	B	C	D	E	F	G
2	H	I	J	K	L	M	N
3	O	P	Q	R	S	T	U
4	V	W	X	Y	Z		

"_ _ _ _ _ WHO _ _ _ _
36 21 31 35 15   24 27 31 42

YOUR _ _ _ _ WILL _ _ _ _ _ _
     27 11 26 15   36 34 37 35 36

IN YOU, _ _ _ _ _ _, LORD,
        16 31 34 44 31 37

HAVE _ _ _ _ _ _ _ _-
     27 15 41 1b 34   16 31 34

_ _ _ _ _ THOSE _ _ _
35 11 24 15 27   42 21 31

_ _ _ _ _ _ _."
35 15 15 24 44 31 37

PSALM 9:10

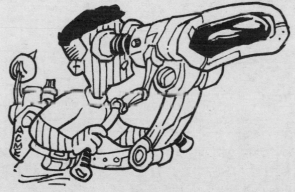

99

COLOR *the* PICTURE

UNFAILING LOVE

"BUT I TRUST IN YOUR UNFAILING LOVE; MY HEART REJOICES IN YOUR SALVATION."

PSALM 13:5

COPY THE ITEMS ABOVE ON THE NEXT PAGE, PLACING THEM IN THE PROPER LOCATION, THEN COLOR THE PICTURE.

SCRAMBLED VERSES

WHAT DOES GOD WANT?

NOT EVERYONE WILL BE OUR FRIEND. AT TIMES THERE WILL BE PROBLEMS WITH OTHER PEOPLE...THEY JUST MAY NOT LIKE US AND SOMETIMES IT WILL BE HARD TO UNDERSTAND WHY.

WHAT WOULD GOD WANT YOU TO DO IN A SITUATION LIKE THIS?

UNSCRAMBLE THE VERSE BELOW AND FIND OUT.

"NI UYO I SRTTU, O YM DGO. OD TNO LTE EM EB TPU OT MSHEA, RNO ETL YM MNEEESI TPHRMUI EORV EM."

"__ ___ ___ _____,
__ ___ ____ ____. ___ ____
___ ___ __ __ _____
__ __ _____ _____,
__ _____ _____
__ _____ ____
__ __."

PSALM 25:2

DOUBLE *the* FUN

UNSCRAMBLE THE UNDERLINED WORDS IN EACH VERSE. ON THE NEXT PAGE, PLACE YOUR ANSWERS IN THE SPACES PROVIDED AND THEN COMPLETE THE CROSSWORD PUZZLE.

1. "SOME TRUST IN OAITHRSC AND SOME IN RHESOS, BUT WE TRUST IN THE MNEA OF THE LORD OUR GOD."

    PSALM 20:7

2. "BUT I SURTT IN YOU, O LORD; I SAY, 'YOU ARE MY GOD.'"

    PSALM 31:14

3. "IN HIM OUR RHESAT JECERIO, FOR WE TRUST IN HIS OYLH NAME."

    PSALM 33:21

1. __ __ __ __ __ __ __

 __ __ __ __ __   __ __ __ __

2. __ __ __ __ __

3. __ __ __ __ __ __   __ __ __ __ __ __ __

 __ __ __ __

105

SCRAMBLED VERSES

LOOK UP THE VERSES BELOW AND PUT THE
WORDS IN THEIR PROPER ORDER.

TOLD HEARTS HAVE PLACE FATHER'S "DO
GOING." YOU HOUSE TRUST MANY YOU, I I
COME WOULD ROOMS; THAT WAY GOING
TROUBLED. PREPARE GOD; YOUR MAY BE SO,
A PLACE WILL BACK I YOU PREPARE AND
TRUST ME. YOU YOU. TO I GO ARE WHERE
KNOW THE WHERE NOT LET AND A PLACE
I AM ALSO IN IN MY TAKE BE WITH AM
IT WERE IN TO THE I AM. TO FOR BE
ME THERE YOU. NOT IF IF FOR AND
ALSO

JOHN 14:1-4

FILL *in the* BLANKS

OVERFLOWING!

BLESSINGS ARE MANY WHEN YOU CHOOSE TO
TRUST IN THE LORD. BUT REALLY TRUSTING
IN GOD IS ONLY POSSIBLE AS YOU ASK HIM
FOR THE POWER TO DO SO.

TRY LETTING GO AND ALLOW GOD TO LEAD
YOU AND WORK OUT ALL THINGS IN YOUR
LIFE.

USING THE WORDS BELOW, COMPLETE THE
VERSE ON THE NEXT PAGE.

OVERFLOW   GOD
HOPE   SPIRIT
PEACE   POWER
TRUST   MAY
HOLY   FILL
HIM   JOY

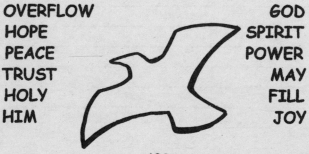

"_____ THE _____ OF _____ _____ YOU WITH ALL _____ AND _____ AS YOU _____ IN _____, SO THAT YOU MAY _____ WITH HOPE BY THE _____ OF THE _____ _____."

ROMANS 15:13

NOW, THAT'S A BLESSING!

SECRET CODES

JEALOUSY AND GREED

A GREAT WAY TO LOSE THE FEELING OF JOY AND PEACE IS TO LET SOMETHING LIKE JEALOUSY OR GREED GAIN A FOOTHOLD IN YOUR LIFE.

NOTHING WILL DAMPEN THE FRUIT OF THE SPIRIT AS FAST AS THESE TWO.

BUT ONCE AGAIN, THE WORD WILL GIVE US GOD'S FEELINGS ON THESE AND THE SOLUTIONS HE HAS TO OVERCOME THEM.

TO SOLVE THE CODED VERSE BELOW, LOOK AT EACH LETTER AND WRITE THE ONE THAT COMES BEFORE IT IN THE ALPHABET.

"LFFQ ZPVS MJWFT GSFF GSPN UIF MPWF PG NPOFZ BOE CF DPOUFOU XJUI XIBU ZPV IBWF, CFDBVTF HPE IBT TBJE, 'OFWFS XJMM J MFBWF ZPV; OFWFS XJMM J GPSTBLF ZPV.'"

HEBREWS 13:5

110

ABCDEFGHIJKLMNOPQRST
UVWXYZ

"————— ————— —————
————— ————— ————
————— ————— ————
——— ————— —————
————— ————— ————,
————— —————
————— —————, —————
——— —— —————
———; ————— —————
—— ——————————————."

FINISH *the* VERSE

AN EVIL R O O T

MONEY IN ITSELF IS NOT EVIL, BUT WHEN A PERSON WANTS MORE AND MORE OF IT, THAT'S WHEN THE TROUBLE BEGINS. WE BEGIN TO LOOK AT WHAT OTHERS HAVE AND START TO BELIEVE THAT WE'VE JUST GOT TO HAVE IT TOO IF WE ARE TO BE HAPPY.

USE THE CODE CHART BELOW TO FINISH THE VERSE. (EG: K=24)

	1	2	3	4	5	6	7
1	A	B	C	D	E	F	G
2	H	I	J	K	L	M	N
3	O	P	Q	R	S	T	U
4	V	W	X	Y	Z		

"__ __ __ THE __ __ __ __ OF
16 31 34   25 31 41 15

__ __ __ __ __ IS A __ __ __ __ OF
26 31 27 15 44   34 31 31 36

ALL __ __ __ __ __ OF __ __ __ __ .
    24 22 27 14 35   15 41 22 25

SOME __ __ __ __ __ __ , __ __ __ __ __
     32 15 31 32 25 15   15 11 17 15 34

FOR __ __ __ __ __ , HAVE __ __ __ -
    26 31 27 15 44   42 11 27

__ __ __ __ __ FROM THE __ __ __ __ __
14 15 34 15 14   16 11 22 36 21

AND __ __ __ __ __ __ __
    32 22 15 34 13 15 14

__ __ __ __ __ __ __ __ __ WITH
36 21 15 26 35 15 25 41 15 35

__ __ __ __ __ __ __ __ __ __ ."
26 11 27 44   17 34 22 15 16 35

1 TIMOTHY 6:10

113

SCRAMBLED VERSES

ABUNDANCE...*or* EMPTINESS?

DO YOU THINK THAT IF YOU HAD EVERY-
THING IN THE WORLD YOU WANTED, YOU
WOULD FINALLY BE HAPPY?

OR WOULD YOU STILL FEEL EMPTY AND
UNSATISFIED?

UNSCRAMBLE THE VERSE BELOW AND FIND
OUT.

"NHET EH ASID OT TMHE, 'TAWHC
TUO! EB NO YRUO ADRUG AASTNGI
LAL NKSDI FO EERDG; A N'SAM EIFL
EDSO   NTO   NSCSITO   NI   ETH
DAUANBCEN FO SHI OSESNSIPSOS.'"

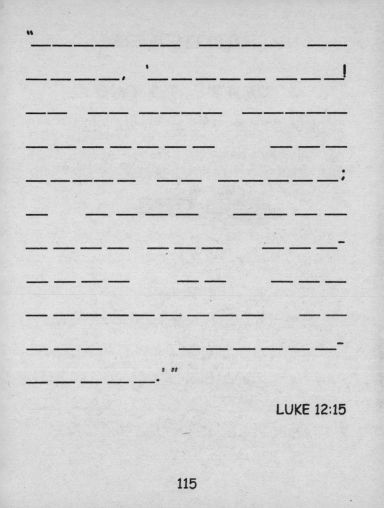

LUKE 12:15

FILL THEM IN

DEATH TO SIN!

LOOK UP COLOSSIANS 3:5 IN YOUR BIBLE.

ON THE NEXT PAGE, FILL IN THE BOXES WITH THE SINS THAT ARE DESERVING OF DEATH.

117

WORD SEARCH

FIND THE WORDS UNDERLINED BELOW IN THE WORD SEARCH ON THE NEXT PAGE.

"BE SHEPHERDS OF GOD'S FLOCK THAT IS IS UNDER YOUR CARE, SERVING AS OVERSEERS—NOT BECAUSE YOU MUST, BUT BECAUSE YOU ARE WILLING, AS GOD WANTS YOU TO BE; NOT GREEDY FOR MONEY, BUT EAGER TO SERVE."

1 PETER 5:2

JUST IN CASE YOU THINK THIS VERSE DOESN'T APPLY TO YOU, THINK AGAIN! AN OVERSEER IS JUST SOMEONE WHO LOOKS OUT FOR THE INTERESTS OF SOMEONE ELSE. MAYBE FOR YOU, IT MIGHT BE A FRIEND OR A YOUNGER BROTHER OR SISTER.

BUT, THE REAL KEY IN THIS VERSE IS BEING *EAGER TO SERVE!*

```
F L O C K D C L D F Q D
G M Z N H S E M D T X Q
N R O G R S A O Z B M J
I H T N D T G L B E C T
V S Z C E T E N H C L H
R D P V B Y R C Q A G M
E C J S E R V E D U B K
S D G Z H B R L D S H X
O V E R S E E R S E L W
N D C F G L P R B L T S
B J A H F M G H R W Z P
H T R P B W K S E B J H
R J E G R E E D Y R C Z
W D Z X R S S H T V D K
H K J B L Y H G D K Q S
```

119

CROSSWORD

TREASURES IN HEAVEN

AVOIDING JEALOUSY OR GREED MEANS TAKING ON A DIFFERENT ATTITUDE. IT'S ABOUT DECIDING ON WHAT WILL HAVE MORE MEANING IN YOUR LIFE.

LET'S SEE WHAT GOD SAYS.

ACROSS
1. "DO NOT STORE UP FOR YOURSELVES _____ ON EARTH."
2. "WHERE MOTH AND _____ DESTROY."
3. "AND WHERE THIEVES BREAK IN AND _____."

MATTHEW 6:19

DOWN
1. "BUT STORE UP FOR _____."
2. "_____ IN HEAVEN."
3. "WHERE MOTH AND RUST DO NOT _____."
4. "AND WHERE _____ DO NOT BREAK IN AND STEAL."
5. "FOR WHERE YOUR TREASURE IS, THERE YOUR _____ WILL BE ALSO."

MATTHEW 6:20-21

121

DOUBLE *the* FUN

UNSCRAMBLE THE UNDERLINED WORDS IN EACH VERSE. ON THE NEXT PAGE, PLACE YOUR ANSWERS IN THE SPACES PROVIDED AND THEN COMPLETE THE CROSSWORD PUZZLE.

SPEAKING TO THE RELIGIOUS LEADERS OF HIS DAY, THE LORD MADE *VERY* CLEAR HIS FEELINGS ON GREED.

1. "'WOE TO YOU, TEACHERS OF THE LAW AND EEPRSSAHI, YOU OPTRYSHECI! YOU LNACE THE OUTSIDE OF THE CUP AND HDSI, BUT INSIDE THEY ARE FULL OF GREED AND SELF-INDULGENCE.'"

   MATTHEW 23:25

2. "THEN THE LORD SAID TO HIM, 'NOW THEN, YOU PHARISEES CLEAN THE SUDOTEI OF THE CUP AND DISH, BUT NSIIED YOU ARE FULL OF REDEG AND WICKEDESS.'"

   LUKE 11:39

1. __ __ __ __ __ __ __

__ __ __ __ __ __ __ __ __ __

__ __ __ __ __ __ __ __ __ __

2. __ __ __ __ __ __ __ __   __ __ __ __ __ __

__ __ __ __ __ __ __

SCRAMBLED VERSES

HAPPINESS

MANY CHASE AFTER HAPPINESS AS IF IT IS THE MOST IMPORTANT THING IN THE WORLD. USUALLY THOUGH, THEY END UP BEING THE MOST *UNHAPPY* PEOPLE AROUND!

HAPPINESS IS A *RESULT*...A RESULT OF MAKING THE RIGHT CHOICES IN LIFE AND LIVING THE KIND OF LIFE GOD WOULD WANT FOR YOU TO LIVE.

LOOK UP THE VERSE BELOW AND PUT THE WORDS IN THEIR PROPER ORDER TO FIND OUT MORE OF WHAT THE LORD SAYS ABOUT HAPPINESS.

GATHERING MAN MEANINGLESS, IS SINNER TOO PLEASES STORING TO WEALTH IT OVER AND UP THE "TO THE PLEASES WISDOM, GOD. WHO CHASING THE ONE WIND." HAPPINESS, HE GIVES OF HAND GOD THE TASK A AFTER BUT WHO HIM, KNOWLEDGE GIVES TO THE TO AND THIS

ECCLESIASTES 2:26

SECRET CODES

A GIFT OF GOD

REAL HAPPINESS COMES FROM GOD FIRST AND WITH WHATEVER HE MAY GIVE IN YOUR LIFE. THIS IS TO BE ENJOYED AS A GRACIOUS GIFT.

TO SOLVE THE CODED VERSE BELOW, LOOK AT EACH LETTER AND WRITE THE ONE THAT COMES BEFORE IT IN THE ALPHABET.

"NPSFPWFS, XIFO HPE HJWFT BOZ NBO XFBMUI BOE QPTTFTTJPOT, BOE FOBCMFT IJN UP FOKPZ UIFN, UP BDDFQU IJT MPU BOE CF IBQQZ JO IJT XPSL — UIJT JT B HJGU PG HPE."

ECCLESIASTES 5:19

126

ABCDEFGHIJKLMNOPQRST
UVWXYZ

"———————————, —————

——— —— ———— —————

——— ———— ——— ————

— ——————— ————————,

——— ——— —— ————

——— —— ————— ————

————, —— ———— ————

——— —— ———— ————

—— —— ———— —— ———

—— —— ———— —— ———

—— —— ——— ———— ———

—— —— —."

FINISH *the* VERSE

A DIFFERENT KIND OF GIFT

DON'T THINK THAT EVERY GIFT IS GIVEN TO YOU FOR YOUR PLEASURE. SOME OF GOD'S GIFTS TO YOU ARE FOR OTHERS.

USE THE CODE CHART BELOW TO FINISH THE VERSE. (EG: K=24)

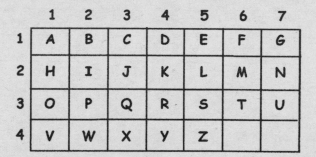

	1	2	3	4	5	6	7
1	A	B	C	D	E	F	G
2	H	I	J	K	L	M	N
3	O	P	Q	R	S	T	U
4	V	W	X	Y	Z		

"EACH ___ ___ ___   ___ ___ ___ ___ ___ ___
       31 27 15   35 21 31 37 25 14

USE ___ ___ ___ ___ ___ ___ ___ ___
    42 21 11 36 15 41 15 34

___ ___ ___ ___ HE HAS ___ ___ -
17 22 16 36   34 15

___ ___ ___ ___ ___ ___ TO ___ ___ ___ ___ ___
13 15 ?? 41 15 14   35 15 34 41 15

___ ___ ___ ___ ___ ___, FAITHFULLY
31 36 21 15 34 35

___ ___ ___ ___ ___ ___ ___ ___ ___ ___ ___ ___
11 14 26 22 27 22 35 36 15 34 22 27 17

GOD'S ___ ___ ___ ___ ___ IN ITS
      17 34 11 13 15

___ ___ ___ ___ ___ ___ ___ ___ ___ ___ ___ ___.
41 11 34 22 31 37 35   16 31 34 26 35

1 PETER 4:10

129

CROSSWORD

HOPE IN GOD

EVEN WHEN YOU FEEL SO LOW, *LOOK TO GOD!*

SOON, HE WILL LIFT YOU UP. **COUNT ON IT!**

ACROSS
1. "WHY ARE YOU _____."
2. "O MY _____?"
3. "WHY SO _____ WITHIN ME?"
4. "PUT YOUR _____ IN GOD."
5. "FOR I WILL YET PRAISE HIM, MY SAVIOR AND MY _____."

DOWN
1. "MY SOUL IS_____ WITHIN ME."
2. "_____ I WILL REMEMBER YOU."
3. "FROM THE _____ OF THE JORDAN."
4. "THE HEIGHTS OF _____ —FROM MOUNT MIZAR."

PSALM 42:5-6

131

FILL *in the* BLANKS

GIVE THANKS

FINALLY, FINDING *TRUE* HAPPINESS DEPENDS ON *YOUR* ATTITUDE TOWARDS EVERYTHING IN YOUR LIFE. WHAT'S THE BEST WAY OF DOING THIS?

USING THE WORDS BELOW, COMPLETE THE VERSES ON THE NEXT PAGE AND YOU'LL SOON FIND OUT!

HEART	LORD
SING	NAME
FATHER	MUSIC
MAKE	THANKS
LORD	EVERYTHING
JESUS	GIVING
GOD	CHRIST

"_____ AND _____ _____

IN YOUR _____ TO THE

_____, ALWAYS _____

_____ TO _____ THE

_____ FOR _____,

IN THE _____ OF OUR _____

_____ _____."

EPHESIANS 5:19-20

133

FINISH *the* VERSE

LONELINESS

IT CAN BE AWFUL, AT TIMES, TO FEEL THAT YOU ARE ALL ALONE; WHEN YOUR FAMILY SEEMS SO BUSY OR WHEN FRIENDS ARE NOT THERE FOR YOU.

BUT, YOU HAVE A **FRIEND** THAT IS ALWAYS WITH YOU AND WITH *HIM,* YOU NEVER NEED TO FEEL LONELY AGAIN!

USE THE CODE CHART BELOW TO FINISH THE VERSES. (EG: K=24)

	1	2	3	4	5	6	7
1	A	B	C	D	E	F	G
2	H	I	J	K	L	M	N
3	O	P	Q	R	S	T	U
4	V	W	X	Y	Z		

"TO ___ ___ ___, O ___ ___ ___ ___, I
   44 31 37   25 31 34 14

___ ___ ___ ___ UP ___ ___   ___ ___ ___ ___ ___."
25 22 16 36   26 44   35 31 37 25

PSALM 25:1

" ___ ___ ___ ___ TO ___ ___ AND BE
  36 37 34 27   26 15

___ ___ ___ ___ ___ ___ ___ ___ TO
17 34 11 13 22 31 37 35

ME, ___ ___ ___ I ___ ___   ___ ___ ___ ___ ___
    16 31 34   11 26   25 31 27 15 25 44

AND ___ ___ ___ ___ ___ ___ ___ ___ ___."
    11 16 16 25 22 13 36 15 14

PSALM 25:16

135

WORD SEARCH

GOD'S CHILDREN...*LONELY?*

IF YOU'RE GOD'S CHILD, HE HAS AN ANSWER FOR LONELINESS. LOOK UP **PSALM 68:6** IN YOUR BIBLE AND YOU'LL FIND OUT WHAT IT IS.

THEN, FIND THE WORDS, LISTED BELOW, IN THE WORD SEARCH ON THE NEXT PAGE.

LIVE

FAMILIES

LONELY

LEADS

LAND

REBELLIOUS

SETS

GOD

SINGING

SUN-SCORCHED

PRISONERS

FORTH

```
T H G T B Z S G D P L W
F Q S I N G I N G G O D
D M B L R X C L O F N N
K S F J E S Q G S H E P
F R U W D A I M R K L R
T R C N L I D S W S Y I
B E P V S E T S P N G S
K B Q L E C Q K D P C O
H E J N I I O R H T F N
M L G Z L J I R Q H L E
L L V R I L D T C Z T R
H I D F M B N L K H Z S
T O V Y A R X F P F E P
S U N E F O R T H T R D
W S C V S N T D N A L G
```

COLOR *the* PICTURE

A FANTASTIC PROMISE!

"AND SURELY I AM WITH YOU ALWAYS, TO THE VERY END OF THE AGE."

MATTHEW 28:20

JESUS HAS PROMISED TO NEVER LEAVE US. NO MATTER WHERE WE ARE OR WHAT WE DO, HE IS *ALWAYS* THERE WITH US.

THE LORD KNOWS OUR NEEDS AND UNDER-STANDS THAT WE NEED COMPANIONSHIP, SO HE HAS GIVEN US OUR FAMILY AND HE HAS GIVEN US FRIENDS.

HE IS SO WORTHY OF OUR PRAISE AND GRATITUDE!

139

DOUBLE *the* FUN

PEACE

UNSCRAMBLE THE UNDERLINED WORDS IN EACH VERSE. ON THE NEXT PAGE, PLACE YOUR ANSWERS IN THE SPACES PROVIDED AND THEN COMPLETE THE CROSSWORD PUZZLE.

1. "I WILL LIE DOWN AND SLEEP IN CPEEA, FOR YOU ALONE, O LORD, MAKE ME DWELL IN YFESAT."

   PSALM 4:8

2. "THE LORD VSIGE STRENGTH TO HIS PEOPLE; THE LORD EBESLSS HIS LPOEPE WITH PEACE."

   PSALM 29:11

3. "TURN FROM EVIL AND DO ODOG; EKSE PEACE AND URPESU IT."

   PSALM 34:14

1. ___ ___ ___ ___   ___ ___ ___ ___ ___

2. ___ ___ ___ ___   ___ ___ ___ ___ ___
   ___ ___ ___ ___ ___

3. ___ ___ ___ ___   ___ ___ ___ ___
   ___ ___ ___ ___ ___ ___

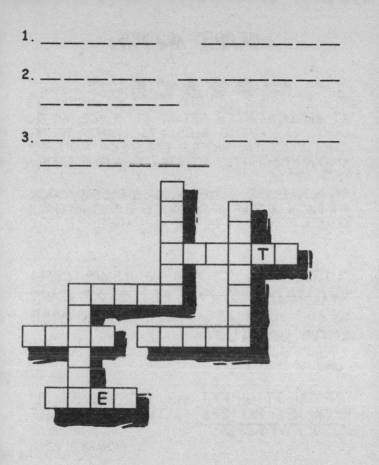

141

SECRET CODES

PEACE...A WAY OF LIFE

IT BEGINS WITH BEING AT PEACE WITH GOD. IN HAVING A RELATIONSHIP WITH THE LORD, HE WOULD LIKE FOR YOU TO KNOW PEACE WITH THOSE IN YOUR LIFE.

TO SOLVE THE CODED VERSES BELOW, LOOK AT EACH LETTER AND WRITE THE ONE THAT COMES BEFORE IT IN THE ALPHABET.

"UIFSFGPSF, TJODF XF IBWF CFFO KVTUJGJFE UISPVHI GBJUI, XF IBWF QFBDF XJUI HPE UISPVHI PVS MPSE KFTVT DISJTU."

ROMANS 5:1

and,

"JG JU JT QPTTJCMF, BT GBS BT JU EFQFOET PO ZPV, MJWF BU QFBDF XJUI FWFSZPOF."

ROMANS 12:18

ABCDEFGHIJKLMNOPQRST
UVWXYZ

"_____ ____ ____ ____ ____ ____ ____ ____,
____ ____ ____ ____ ____ ____ ____
____ ____ ____ ____ ____ ____ ____
____ ____ ____ ____ ____ ____,
____ ____ ____ ____ ____ ____
____ ____ ____ ____ ____ ____
____ ____ ____ ____ ____ ____ ____
____ ____ ____ ____ ____."

"_____ ____ ____ ____ ____ ____ -
____ ____ ____ ____, ____ ____ ____ ____
____ ____ ____ ____ ____ ____
____ ____ ____ ____, ____ ____ ____ ____
____ ____ ____ ____ ____
____ ____ ____ ____ ____."

CROSSWORD

SOWING PEACE

ACROSS

1. "BUT THE _____."
2. "THAT COMES FROM _____."
3. "IS FIRST OF ALL _____."
4. "THEN _____ -LOVING, CONSIDERATE."

DOWN

1. "_____, FULL OF MERCY AND GOOD FRUIT."
2. "IMPARTIAL AND _____."
3. "PEACEMAKERS WHO SOW IN _____."
4. "RAISE A _____ OF RIGHTEOUSNESS."

JAMES 3:17–18

145

FILL *in the* BLANKS

PeAce RuLeS!

ASK JESUS TO *RULE* IN YOUR HEART, TO BE LORD IN YOUR LIFE, AND YOU WILL KNOW HIS PEACE. THEN, **HIS** PEACE WILL FLOW OUT OF YOU TO OTHERS.

USING THE WORDS BELOW, COMPLETE THE VERSES ON THE NEXT PAGE AND YOU'LL KNOW WHAT TO DO.

QUARRELS	FOOLISH
PEACE	MEMBERS
RIGHTEOUSNESS	DESIRES
FLEE	ARGUMENTS
LORD	PURSUE
LOVE	HEART
YOUTH	PEACE
CHRIST	BODY
HEARTS	PEACE

"LET THE _____ OF _____ RULE IN YOUR _____, SINCE AS _____ OF ONE _____ YOU WERE CALLED TO _____."

COLOSSIANS 3:15

"_____ THE EVIL _____ OF _____, AND _____ _____, FAITH, _____ AND _____, ALONG WITH THOSE WHO CALL ON THE _____ OUT OF A PURE _____. DON'T HAVE ANYTHING TO DO WITH _____ AND STUPID _____, BECAUSE YOU KNOW THEY PRODUCE _____."

2 TIMOTHY 2:22-23

FILL THEM IN

DON'T BE ANXIOUS!

LOOK UP PHILIPPIANS 4:6-7 IN YOUR BIBLE.

ON THE NEXT PAGE, FILL IN THE BOXES WITH WHAT YOU NEED TO DO AND WHAT YOU WILL RECEIVE.

SCRAMBLED VERSES

TAKE HEART!

GOD GIVES SO MUCH. THE PEACE THAT HE LEAVES WITH US IS ONE OF THE BEST THINGS WE CAN HAVE. TO BE FREE OF ANXIETY AND WORRY IS A WONDERFUL FEELING.

UNSCRAMBLE THE VERSES BELOW AND BE ASSURED!

"CEEPA I EVLAE WHTI UYO; YM PCAEE I IGVE OYU. I OD TON VIEG OT YOU SA HET LWRDO IESGV. OD TNO TLE OYRU THAERS EB UOEDBTLR NDA OD ONT EB AAIFDR."

"I AVHE DTLO OUY SEEHT SHIGNT, OS HATT NI EM UYO YMA AVHE CEAPE. NI SITH ODRWL UYO LILW AEVH BLRTEUO. TBU TEKA ARHET! I EAVH COEORVEM HET DWLOR."

"
————— — ————— —————— —————

—————— —————; —— —————— —————

— —————— ————. —————— —————

————— —————— ——— ——————

——— —————— ——— —————————

——— —————————. —— —————— ———

——— —————— ————— —————————

——— —— ————— —————— ————— —————

——————— ——————."

"
—— ——— ————— ————— —————

—————— ————— —————————, ———

———— —— —— ————

——— ——————— ————— —————————.

—— — ——————— ————— ——

————— ————— ————— ————— —— ——

—————————. ————— —————

—————————! —— ————— —————-

————— ————— —————————."

FINISH the VERSE

TEMPTATION!

DOES A DAY GO BY WHERE THERE ISN'T A TEMPTATION TO DO SOMETHING WRONG OR TO REACT IN THE WRONG WAY?

YOU WANT TO LIVE RIGHT...YOU WANT TO DO AS GOD WOULD HAVE YOU DO, BUT SOME-TIMES, IT ALMOST SEEMS IMPOSSIBLE. IS THERE *ANY* HELP?

LET'S LOOK TO GOD'S WORD, ONCE AGAIN.

USE THE CODE CHART BELOW TO FINISH THE VERSE. (EG: K=24)

	1	2	3	4	5	6	7
1	A	B	C	D	E	F	G
2	H	I	J	K	L	M	N
3	O	P	Q	R	S	T	U
4	V	W	X	Y	Z		

"WHEN ___ ___ ___ ___ ___ ___ ___, NO ONE
36 15 26 32 36 15 14

___ ___ ___ ___ ___ ___ SAY, 'GOD IS
35 21 31 37 25 14

___ ___ ___ ___ ___ ___ ___ ___ ME.' FOR GOD
36 15 26 32 36 22 27 17

___ ___ ___ ___ ___ ___ BE ___ ___ ___ ___ ___ ___
13 11 27 27 31 36   36 15 26 32 36 15 14

BY ___ ___ ___ ___, NOR DOES HE ___ ___ ___ ___ ___
   15 41 22 25   36 15 26 32 36

___ ___ ___ ___ ___ ___; BUT ___ ___ ___ ___ ONE
11 27 44 31 27 15   15 11 13 21

IS ___ ___ ___ ___ ___ ___ ___ WHEN, BY HIS
   36 15 26 32 36 15 14

___ ___ ___ ___ ___ ___ ___ ___ ___ ___ ___ ___,
31 42 27   15 41 22 25   14 15 35 22 34 15

HE IS ___ ___ ___ ___ ___ ___ ___ AWAY
      14 34 11 17 17 15 14

AND ___ ___ ___ ___ ___ ___ ___ THEN,
    15 27 36 22 13 15 14

AFTER ___ ___ ___ ___ ___ ___ HAS
      14 15 35 22 34 15

___ ___ ___ ___ ___ ___ ___ ___ ___, IT GIVES
13 31 27 13 15 22 41 15 14

___ ___ ___ ___ ___ ___ TO ___ ___ ___; AND SIN,
12 22 34 36 21   35 22 27

WHEN IT IS ___ ___ ___ ___ - ___ ___ ___ ___ ___,
           16 37 25 25   17 34 31 42 27

GIVES ___ ___ ___ ___ ___ ___ TO ___ ___ ___ ___ ___ ___."
      12 22 34 36 21   14 15 11 36 21

JAMES 1:13-15

153

WORD SEARCH

STAND AGAINST TEMPTATION

DOES GOD HAVE A WAY FOR YOU TO RESIST TEMPTATION?

FIND THE WORDS UNDERLINED BELOW IN THE WORD SEARCH ON THE NEXT PAGE.

"NO TEMPTATION HAS SEIZED YOU EXCEPT WHAT IS COMMON TO MAN. AND GOD IS FAITHFUL; HE WILL NOT LET YOU BE TEMPTED BEYOND WHAT YOU CAN BEAR. BUT WHEN YOU ARE TEMPTED, HE WILL ALSO PROVIDE A WAY OUT SO THAT YOU CAN STAND UP UNDER IT."

1 CORINTHIANS 10:13

```
X R Z G O D R L F R N J
F W D G S E I Z E D L Z
B H J T P D T H T R W K
E K L D E S E L H A B T
A M T N C M M M Y T L C
R B H N R T P S D U R M
F R Q P D T T T F F D P
S T A N D K A H E H X E
B E J J N L T B C D M X
K D T K B I I N T U R C
H I L T A D O N D N G E
L V T F N M N N Q D Z P
T O C V M J A T D E L T
H R P O H L G N K R T X
T P C R B B E Y O N D S
```

155

MULTIPLE CHOICE

"PEOPLE WHO WANT TO GET RICH FALL INTO TEMPTATION AND A TRAP AND INTO MANY FOOLISH AND HARMFUL DESIRES THAT PLUNGE MEN INTO RUIN AND DESTRUCTION."

1 TIMOTHY 6:9

AFTER READING THE VERSE ABOVE, WHAT WOULD BE THE RIGHT CHOICES BELOW?

1. YOU GET A LOT OF MONEY FOR YOUR BIRTH DAY.

    A) YOU HIDE IT AWAY, SO YOU DON'T EVER HAVE TO SHARE.

    B) YOU GIVE SOME BACK TO GOD, PUT SOME TOWARDS SAVINGS, AND TAKE A LITTLE TO SPEND.

    C) YOU SPEND IT ALL AT THE LOCAL VIDEO ARCADE.

2. YOUR YOUNGER BROTHER'S BIKE HAS A FLAT
   TIRE AND HE HAS NO MONEY TO REPAIR IT.
   - A) YOU OFFER TO LOAN HIM THE MONEY
     AND HE CAN PAY IT BACK WHEN HE
     CAN.
   - B) YOU TELL HIM TO TAKE CARE OF HIS
     OWN PROBLEMS.
   - C) YOU GIVE HIM THE MONEY AS LONG
     AS HE CLEANS YOUR ROOM FOR THE
     NEXT YEAR.

3. YOU FINALLY GOT THAT NEW GAME SYSTEM!
   - A) YOU SHARE IT WITH NO ONE.
   - B) YOU SPEND ALL YOUR TIME AT IT...
     YOUR CHORES AREN'T GETTING DONE
     AND YOUR GRADES ARE SLIPPING.
   - C) YOU CAREFULLY SCHEDULE YOUR
     TIME ON IT.

4. YOU'VE BEEN ASKED AT CHURCH TO GIVE TO
   AN EMERGENCY RELIEF FUND.
   - A) YOU GIVE TEN PERCENT OF YOUR
     SAVINGS.
   - B) YOU'RE ANGRY BUT GIVE BECAUSE IT
     IS EXPECTED OF YOU.
   - C) YOU ASK GOD WHAT AMOUNT HE
     WOULD HAVE YOU GIVE.

SECRET CODES

WE WILL FIND MERCY AND HELP

BE CONFIDENT! NO MATTER WHAT YOU'VE DONE, IT DOESN'T CHANGE GOD'S LOVE FOR YOU. YOU *CAN* GO TO HIM AND FIND THAT HIS FORGIVENESS IS ALWAYS THERE FOR YOU. HE WILL GIVE THE STRENGTH YOU NEED TO WITHSTAND TEMPTATION.

TO SOLVE THE CODED VERSES BELOW, LOOK AT EACH LETTER AND WRITE THE ONE THAT COMES BEFORE IT IN THE ALPHABET.

"CFDBVTF IF IJNTFMG TVGGFSFE XIFO IF XBT UFNQUFE, IF JT BCMF UP IFMQ UIPTF XIP BSF CFJOH UFNQUFE."

HEBREWS 2:18

"MFU VT UIFO BQQSPBDI UIF UISPOF PG HSBDF XJUI DPOGJEFODF, TP UIBU XF NBZ SFDFJWF NFSDZ BOE GJOE HSBDF UP IFMQ VT JO PVS UJNF PG OFFE."

HEBREWS 4:16

158

A B C D E F G H I J K L M N O P Q R S T
U V W X Y Z

"

"

"

"

FILL *in the* BLANKS

WATCH YOURSELF!

NOT ONLY DO WE DEAL WITH OUR OWN SIN,
BUT THERE ARE THE SINS OF OTHERS THAT
MAY AFFECT US IN SOME WAY. HOW DO WE
HANDLE THAT?

USING THE WORDS BELOW, COMPLETE THE
VERSE ON THE NEXT PAGE AND YOU'LL KNOW
WHAT TO DO.

WATCH	BROTHERS
TEMPTED	RESTORE
CAUGHT	GENTLY
SOMEONE	ALSO
SPIRITUAL	SIN
YOURSELF	SHOULD

"_____, IF _____
IS _____ IN A _____, YOU
WHO ARE _____
_____ _____ HIM
_____. BUT _____
_____, OR YOU _____
MAY BE _____."

GALATIANS 6:1

CROSSWORD

PATIENCE

THEY SAY, "PATIENCE IS A VIRTUE"...AND IT IS, BUT SOMETIMES, IT SURE SEEMS TO BE A VERY DIFFICULT THING TO DO!

ACROSS

1. "_____ AS AN EXAMPLE OF PATIENCE."
2. "IN THE FACE OF _____."
3. "TAKE THE _____ WHO SPOKE."
4. "IN THE _____ OF THE LORD."

DOWN

1. "AS YOU KNOW, WE CONSIDER _____."
2. "THOSE WHO HAVE _____."
3. "YOU HAVE HEARD OF _____ PERSEVERANCE."
4. "AND HAVE _____ WHAT THE LORD FINALLY BROUGHT ABOUT."
5. "THE LORD IS FULL OF COMPASSION AND _____."

JAMES 5:10-11

FILL THEM IN

AN EXAMPLE

AFTER GETTING THROUGH THESE VERSES, YOU MIGHT FIND IT A LITTLE EASIER TO BE PATIENT ABOUT THE THINGS THAT MAY HAPPEN IN YOUR LIFE.

LOOK UP 2 CORINTHIANS 6:3-6 IN YOUR BIBLE.

ON THE NEXT PAGE, FILL IN THE BOXES WITH THESE EXAMPLES OF SUFFERINGS AND GODLY RESPONSES.

165

FINISH *the* VERSE

PATIENT SALVATION

GOD'S PATIENCE HAS MEANT FOR US, OUR
SALVATION. SURELY, THE LORD WOULD WANT
US TO SHOW OTHERS PATIENCE WHEN THEY
DISSAPOINT US.

USE THE CODE CHART BELOW TO FINISH THE
VERSE. (EG: K=24)

	1	2	3	4	5	6	7
1	A	B	C	D	E	F	G
2	H	I	J	K	L	M	N
3	O	P	Q	R	S	T	U
4	V	W	X	Y	Z		

"_ _ _ _ IN _ _ _ _ THAT
 12 15 11 34   26 22 27 14

OUR _ _ _ _ _ ' _ _ _-
     25 31 34 14 35   32 11

_ _ _ _ _ _ MEANS _ _ _-
36 22 15 27 13 15   35 11 25

_ _ _ _ _ _ , JUST AS OUR
41 11 36 22 31 27

DEAR _ _ _ _ _ _ _
      12 34 31 36 21 15 34

_ _ _ _ ALSO _ _ _ _ _
32 11 37 25   42 34 31 36 15

YOU WITH THE _ _ _ _ _ _
             42 22 35 14 31 26

THAT _ _ _ GAVE HIM."
     17 31 14

2 PETER 3:15

167

COLOR *the* PICTURE

A LAST WORD

THE APOSTLE PAUL SPOKE TO ALL OF US IN PHILIPPIANS 2:14-18 AND THEY ARE GOOD WORDS TO LEAVE YOU WITH.

MAY GOD'S BLESSINGS GO WITH YOU.

"DO EVERYTHING WITHOUT COMPLAINING OR ARGUING, SO THAT YOU MAY BECOME BLAMELESS AND PURE, CHILDREN OF GOD WITHOUT FAULT IN A CROOKED AND DEPRAVED GENERATION, IN WHICH YOU SHINE LIKE STARS IN THE UNIVERSE AS YOU HOLD OUT THE WORD OF LIFE—IN ORDER THAT I MAY BOAST ON THE DAY OF CHRIST THAT I DID NOT RUN OR LABOR FOR NOTHING. BUT EVEN IF I AM BEING POURED OUT LIKE A DRINK OFFERING ON THE SACRIFICE AND SERVICE COMING FROM YOUR FAITH, I AM GLAD AND REJOICE WITH ALL OF YOU. SO YOU TOO SHOULD BE GLAD AND REJOICE WITH ME."

```
H R Q L Y V D M F K F W
F J G O N C L G A E F B
G S J V B T B X B W A L
A D E E D F L X O T R A
A N T F E L Q S O R F D
T P G R B W C X U R S X
R Z T E R V D H A Y S G
W A C T R B D M D M E W
H A P P I N E S S P N L
Q L R V B J D Z B D I D
M W I B B B E K C F L Q
B Y D N B C T W T H E J
T C E P A Q N S N K N W
N M J E B V S M Q B O P
K R P D B R D G U I L T
```

PG. 9

"LET US THEN __APPROACH__ THE __THRONE__ OF GRACE WITH __CONFIDENCE__, SO THAT WE MAY __RECEIVE__ __MERCY__ AND FIND __GRACE__ TO __HELP__ US IN OUR __TIME__ OF __NEED__."

HEBREWS 4:16

PG. 11

"COME TO ME, ALL YOU WHO ARE WEARY AND BURDENED, AND I WILL GIVE YOU REST. TAKE MY YOKE UPON YOU AND LEARN FROM ME, FOR I AM GENTLE AND HUMBLE IN HEART. AND YOU WILL FIND REST FOR YOUR SOULS. FOR MY YOKE IS EASY AND MY BUR-DEN IS LIGHT."

MATTHEW 11:28-30

170

ABCDEFGHIJKLMNOPQRS
TUVWXYZ

"FOR THE WAGES
OF SIN IS
DEATH, BUT
THE GIFT OF
GOD IS ETER-
NAL LIFE IN
CHRIST JESUS
OUR LORD."

ROMANS 6:23

"SO I SAY, LIVE
35 11 44   25 22 41 15
BY THE SPIRIT, AND
        35 32 22 34 22 36
YOU WILL NOT
        42 22 25 25
GRATIFY THE
17 34 11 36 16 44
DESIRES OF THE
14 15 22 34 15 35
SINFUL NATURE."
35 22 27 16 37 25 27 11 36 37 34 15

GALATIANS 5:16

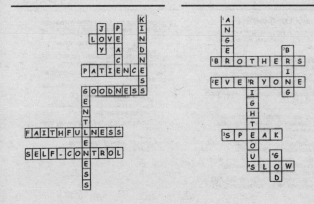

1. <u>B E D S</u>   <u>H E A R T S</u>
2. <u>A N G E R</u>   <u>M O M E N T</u>
3. <u>F O R G A V E</u>   <u>T I M E</u>
   <u>W R A T H</u>

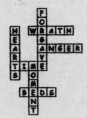

MULTIPLE CHOICE

ANGER IS JUST A FEELING, BUT IT IS WHAT YOU DO WITH IT THAT CAN MAKE IT RIGHT OR WRONG.

1. YOUR BROTHER CALLS YOU A NAME. WHAT SHOULD YOU DO?
   A) CALL HIM AN EVEN NASTIER NAME.
   B) TELL HIM THAT WASN'T NICE AND THAT YOU DIDN'T LIKE IT.
   C) IGNORE HIM AND DON'T SPEAK TO HIM AGAIN.

2. YOU WANT TO STAY OVERNIGHT AT A FRIEND'S HOUSE. YOUR PARENTS SAY NO.
   A) YOU SHOULD ARGUE WITH THEM.
   B) YOU SHOULD HAVE A TEMPER TANTRUM.
   C) YOU SHOULD ACCEPT THEIR ANSWER AND MAKE OTHER PLANS.

3. A FRIEND SHARES HER CANDY WITH EVERYONE ELSE, BUT LEAVES YOU OUT.
   A) CALL HER NAMES.
   B) TALK ABOUT HER BEHIND HER BACK.
   C) TELL HER PRIVATELY HOW YOU FEEL.

---

4. JUST BEFORE IT'S YOUR TURN IN THE HOT DOG LINE, SOMEONE BUTTS IN FRONT OF YOU.
   A) YELL AT THEM AND TELL THEM YOU'RE NEXT.
   B) POLITELY TELL THEM YOU ARE NEXT.
   C) PUSH THEM OUT OF THE WAY.

5. THE TEACHER EMBARRASSES YOU IN FRONT OF THE CLASS.
   A) TALK POLITELY WITH THE TEACHER AFTER CLASS.
   B) EMBARRASS THE TEACHER BACK.
   C) AFTER CLASS, PUT TACKS ON THE TEACHER'S CHAIR.

6. YOU SEE A GROUP OF KIDS PICKING ON YOUR FRIEND.
   A) RUN IN WITH FISTS FLYING.
   B) GO TO AN ADULT FOR HELP.
   C) GO STAND BESIDE YOUR FRIEND.

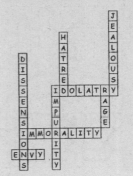

"IN YOUR ANGER
DO NOT SIN: DO
NOT LET THE SUN
GO DOWN WHILE
YOU ARE STILL
ANGRY, AND DO
NOT GIVE THE
DEVIL A FOOT-
HOLD."

"GET RID OF ALL
BITTERNESS,
RAGE AND ANGER,
BRAWLING AND
SLANDER, ALONG
WITH EVERY
FORM OF MALICE.
BE KIND AND
COMPASSIONATE
TO ONE ANOTHER
FORGIVING EACH
OTHER, JUST AS
IN CHRIST GOD
FORGAVE YOU."

"A FOOL GIVES FULL
   11 11 11 14   18 27 22 25
VENT TO HIS ANGER,
41 15 27 36   11 27 17 34
BUT A WISE MAN
          42 22 35 15   26 11 27
KEEPS HIMSELF
          21 27 26 35 15 25 16
UNDER CONTROL."
          13 31 27 36 34 31 25

PROVERBS 29:11

"THEREFORE, AS GOD'S CHOSEN
PEOPLE, HOLY AND DEARLY LOVED,
CLOTHE YOURSELVES WITH
COMPASSION, KINDNESS,
HUMILITY GENTLENESS AND
PATIENCE. BEAR WITH EACH OTHER
AND FORGIVE WHATEVER
GRIEVANCES YOU MAY HAVE
AGAINST ONE ANOTHER. FORGIVE
AS THE LORD FORGAVE YOU."

COLOSSIANS 3:12-13

173

"BLESS THOSE WHO PERSECUTE YOU; BLESS AND DO NOT CURSE. REJOICE WITH THOSE WHO REJOICE; MOURN WITH THOSE WHO MOURN. LIVE IN HARMONY WITH ONE ANOTHER. DO NOT BE PROUD, BUT BE WILLING TO ASSOCIATE WITH PEOPLE OF LOW POSITION. DO NOT BE CONCEITED."

ROMANS 12:14-16

```
K M W I B B C T I N B O
F B Y D B A Q N N Q S L
T C O N C E I T T U H W
O T H E R S T D I E K O B
K K C P D V D T R E U L
H R Q O Y C L G E M L R
F J G O N T B X S R D D
G S J V B K F L T R T A
S D B E O L E S S I S M
P E T O R B V D H P T B
T A L H U M I L I T Y I
R Z T F B B D M S D N T
W A C T I N E S B F I I
H A P P B S Q Z C H L O
Q L R V B P H K T K N N
```

"BROTHERS, IF
 12 34 31 36 21 15 34 35
SOMEONE IS
 35 31 . 26 15 31 27 15
CAUGHT INA SIN, YOU
 13 11 37 17 21 36   35 22 37
WHO ARE SPIRITUAL
            35 32 22 34 22 36 37 11 25
SHOULD RESTORE
 35 21 31 37 25 14 14 15 35 36 31 34 15
HIM GENTLY. BUT
      17 15 27 36 25 44
WATCH YOURSELF, OR YOU
 47 11 36 13 21
ALSO MAY BE TEMPTED.
 11 25 35 31   36 15 26 37 36 15 21
CARRY EACH OTHERS
 13 11 34 34 44 15 11 13 21
BURDENS, AND IN THIS
 12 37 34 21 27 35   36 21 27 35
WAY YOU WILL FULFILL
            16 37 25 16 22 25 25
THE LAW OF CHRIST."
     25 11 47 13 21 34 22 35 36

GALATIANS 6:1-2

1. MERCY   LOVE
2. GRACIOUS
   RIGHTEOUS
3. LORD
   COMPASSION

ABCDEFGHIJKLMNOPQRST
UVWXYZ

"ABOVE ALL, LOVE
EACH OTHER
DEEPLY, BE-
CAUSE LOVE
COVERS OVER
A MULTITUDE OF
SINS. OFFER
HOSPITALITY
TO ONE ANOTHER
WITHOUT GRUMB-
LING."

1 PETER 4:8-9

" FINALLY , ALL OF YOU, LIVE
IN HARMONY WITH ONE
ANOTHER; BE SYMPATHETIC , LOVE
AS BROTHERS , BE COMPASSIONATE
AND HUMBLE . DO NOT REPAY
EVIL WITH EVIL OR INSULT WITH
INSULT , BUT WITH BLESSING ,
BECAUSE TO THIS YOU WERE CALLED
SO THAT YOU MAY INHERIT A
BLESSING ."

1 PETER 3:8-9

"THERE ARE S I X THINGS THE
LORD HATES,
SEVEN THAT ARE
DETESTABLE TO
HIM: HAUGHTY EYES, A
LYING TONGUE, HANDS
THAT SHED INNOCENT
BLOOD, A HEART THAT
DEVISES WICKED
SCHEMES, FEET
THAT ARE QUICK TO RUSH
INTO EVIL, A FALSE WITNESS
WHO POURS OUT LIES AND A
MAN WHO STIRS UP DIS-
SENSION AMONG
BROTHERS."

PROVERBS 6:16-19

"YOU ARE NOT A
GOD WHO TAKES
PLEASURE IN
EVIL; WITH YOU
THE WICKED CAN-
NOT DWELL. THE
ARROGANT CAN-
NOT STAND IN
YOUR PRESENCE;
YOU HATE ALL
WHO DO WRONG-

PSALM 5:4-5

-THERE IS A TIME FOR EVERYTHING AND A SEASON FOR EVERY ACTIVITY UNDER HEAVEN.-

ECCLESIASTES 3:1

-A TIME TO LOVE AND A TIME TO HATE.-

ECCLESIASTES 3:8

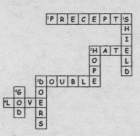

"BUT I TELL YOU WHO HEAR ME: LOVE YOUR ENEMIES, DO GOOD TO THOSE WHO HATE YOU, BLESS THOSE WHO CURSE YOU, PRAY FOR THOSE WHO MISTREAT YOU."

LUKE 6:27-28

176

HOW DOES GOD LOVE US?

"FOR G O D SO L O V E D
17 31 14   25 31 41 15 14

THE W O R L D THAT HE
42 31 34 25 14

G A V E HIS O N E
17 31 15 21 31 14

AND O N L Y S O N, THAT
31 27 25 44 35 31 27

W H O E V E R BELIEVES I N
42 21 31 14 35 14 27   22 27

H I M S H A L L NOT
21 22 24 31 21 25 25

P E R I S H BUT HAVE
32 15 34 27 11 21

E T E R N A L L I F E."
15 36 15 34 27 11 25   25 22 16 15

JOHN 3:16

MAYBE, IF WE CHOOSE TO TREAT OTHERS KINDLY,
NO MATTER WHAT, OR WE DO AS ASKED, OUR *ACT*
OF OBEDIANCE DEMONSTRATES OUR LOVE!

A B C D E F G H I J K L M N O P Q R S T
U V W X Y Z

"A N E W C O M M A N D
I G I V E   Y O U:
L O V E   O N E
A N O T H E R, A S I
H A V E   L O V E D
Y O U, S O   Y O U
M U S T L O V E   O N E
A N O T H E R. B Y
T H I S A L L M E N
W I L L K N O W T H A T
Y O U A R E M Y D I S-
C I P L E S. I F Y O U
L O V E   O N E   A N O-
T H E R."

JOHN 13:34-35

MULTIPLE CHOICE

"YOU HAVE HEARD THAT IT WAS SAID, 'LOVE
YOUR NEIGHBOR AND HATE YOUR ENEMY.'
BUT I TELL YOU: LOVE YOUR ENEMIES AND
PRAY FOR THOSE WHO PERSECUTE YOU."

MATTHEW 5:43-44

BASED ON THE VERSES ABOVE, WHAT SHOULD
BE DONE IN THE FOLLOWING SITUATIONS?

1. A GIRL AT SCHOOL HAS BEEN SPREADING
LIES ABOUT YOU.
   A) CHALLENGE HER TO A FIGHT.
   B) INVITE HER TO YOUR HOUSE AND
   GET TO KNOW HER.
   C) REPORT HER TO THE PRINCIPAL.

2. SOMEONE STOLE YOUR BIKE AND YOU
KNOW WHO IT IS.
   A) PHONE THE POLICE.
   B) ASK FOR IT BACK AND OFFER YOUR
   OLD BIKE FOR FREE.
   C) YOU AND YOUR BUDDIES SHOULD GO
   AND CONFRONT HIM.

3. SOMEONE YOU THOUGHT WAS YOUR
FRIEND COPIED YOUR BOOK REPORT AND
HAS BLAMED YOU FOR CHEATING.
   A) GOD REVEALS THE TRUTH AND YOU
   DECIDE YOU CAN NO LONGER BE
   FRIENDS.
   B) YOU TAKE THE BLAME.
   C) GOD REVEALS THE TRUTH AND YOU
   OFFER FORGIVENESS.

4. KIDS AT SCHOOL LAUGH AT YOU BECAUSE
OF YOUR FAITH.
   A) IN THE FUTURE, YOU DECIDE TO
   KEEP YOUR FAITH A SECRET.
   B) YOU DECIDE TO USE THIS AS AN
   OPPORTUNITY TO SHARE YOUR
   FAITH.
   C) YOU BOLDLY CONFRONT THEM AND
   CONDEMN THEM FOR THEIR SIN.

5. JESUS WAS UNFAIRLY JUDGED AND SENT
TO THE CROSS.
   A) HE ASKED HIS FATHER TO FORGIVE
   THOSE RESPONSIBLE, THEN DIED
   FOR US ALL.
   B) HE CALLED UPON LEGIONS OF
   ANGELS TO SAVE HIM.
   C) HE CRIED OUT FOR MERCY.

1. S T R E N G T H
2. G O O D N E S S   L O V E
   L I F E   D W E L L
   H O U S E
3. R E S T   H O P E

- BUT LOVE YOUR ENEMIES, DO GOOD TO THEM, AND LEND TO THEM WITHOUT EXPECTING TO GET ANYTHING BACK. THEN YOUR REWARD WILL BE GREAT, AND YOU WILL BE SONS OF THE MOST HIGH, BECAUSE HE IS KIND TO THE UNGRATEFUL AND WICKED."

LUKE 6:35

Across/Down: IMITATORS, CHILDREN, AND, CHRIST, HIMSELF, FRAGRANCE, SACRIFICE

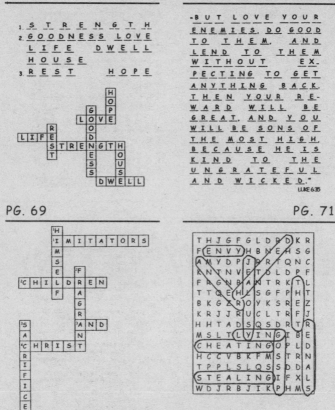

178

MULTIPLE CHOICE

"DO TO OTHERS AS YOU WOULD HAVE THEM DO TO YOU."

LUKE 6:31

AFTER READING THE VERSE ABOVE, WHAT WOULD BE THE RIGHT CHOICES BELOW?

1. PETER BETRAYED JESUS THE NIGHT OF HIS TRIAL.
   A) JESUS FOREVER BANNED HIM FROM HEAVEN.
   B) JESUS EXPECTED PETER TO MAKE IT UP TO HIM.
   C) JESUS FORGAVE HIM.

2. JESUS TOLD OF A MAN WHO WAS FORGIVEN HIS DEBTS.
   A) THE MAN WAS NOW FREE TO COLLECT FROM THOSE WHO OWED HIM.
   B) HE SHOULD FORGIVE OTHERS THEIR DEBTS TO HIM.
   C) HE SHOULD PAY IT BACK ANYWAY.

3. BOTH YOU AND YOUR FRIEND HAVE BEEN OFFERED THE SAME ROLE IN THE SCHOOL PLAY.
   A) DO YOUR BEST AT THE AUDITION.
   B) OFFER A BRIBE TO GET THE PART.
   C) DECLINE THE PART.

4. JESUS TOLD OF A FATHER WHO WAITED FOR A REBELLIOUS SON TO RETURN HOME.
   A) THE FATHER SHOULD WELCOME HIM BACK AND CELEBRATE.
   B) HE SHOULD NOT ALLOW THE SON BACK UNTIL HE PAYS BACK THE MONEY HE SQUANDERED.
   C) HE SHOULD TAKE HIM BACK BUT TREAT HIM AS ONE OF HIS SERVANTS.

5. AN INJURED MAN LIES ON THE SIDE OF THE ROAD.
   A) PASS BY, HOPING SOMEONE ELSE WILL TAKE CARE OF HIM.
   B) MAKE HIM COMFORTABLE, THEN RUN FOR HELP.
   C) CHECK HIS CLOTHING FOR ANY VALUABLES.

6. YOUR PARENTS HAVE ASKED A FAVOR, THAT YOU WOULD CLEAN THE CARS.
   A) YOU AGREE BUT DECIDE LATER NOT TO BOTHER.
   B) YOU WILL...AS LONG AS THEY PAY YOU.
   C) YOU DO IT WILLINGLY, REALIZING HOW MUCH THEY DO FOR YOU.

PG. 75

"IF YOU L O V E THOSE WHO
　　　25 31 41 15

L O V E YOU, WHAT C R E D I T
25 31 41 15　　　　　13 14 15 14 22 36

IS T H A T TO YOU? EVEN
　　36 21 11 36

'S I N N E R S' L O V E
38 22 27 27 19 34 35　　29 31 41 15

T H O S E WHO L O V E
36 21 31 35 15　　　　25 31 41 15

THEM. AND IF YOU DO G O O D TO
　　　　　　　　　　　　17 31 31 7

T H O S E WHO ARE G O O D
36 21 31 35 15　　　　　17 31 31 7

TO YOU. WHAT C R E D I T IS
　　　　　　　13 14 15 14 22 36

THAT TO Y O U? EVEN
　　　　　44 31 37

'S I N N E R S' DO THAT.
35 22 27 27 19 34 35

LUKE 6:32-33

" DO NOT GLOAT WHEN
YOUR ENEMY FALLS ;
WHEN HE STUMBLES ,
DO NOT LET YOUR
HEART REJOICE ."

" BLESS THOSE WHO
PERSECUTE YOU ;
BLESS AND DO NOT
CURSE ."

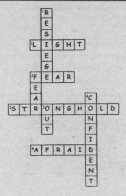

"KEEP YOUR LIVES FREE
FROM THE LOVE OF MONEY
AND BE CONTENT WITH
WHAT YOU HAVE , BECAUSE
GOD HAS SAID, ' NEVER WILL
I LEAVE YOU ; NEVER WILL
I FORSAKE YOU .'"
HEBREWS 13:5

A B C D E F G H I J K L M N O P Q R S T
U V W X Y Z
" CAST YOUR CARES
ON THE LORD AND
HE WILL SUSTAIN
YOU ; HE WILL
NEVER LET THE
RIGHTEOUS FALL ."

" BUT YOU, O GOD,
WILL BRING DOWN
THE WICKED INTO
THE PIT OF COR-
RUPTION ; BLOOD-
THIRSTY AND
DECEITFUL MEN
WILL NOT LIVE
OUT HALF THEIR
DAYS, BUT AS FOR
ME, I TRUST IN
YOU ."

1. F E A R   P U R E
   F O R E V E R
   O R D I N A N C E S

2. W A L K   V A L L E Y
   S H A D O W   E V I L
   R O D   C O M F O R T

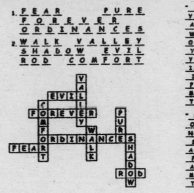

" THEREFORE I TELL
YOU DO NOT WORRY
ABOUT YOUR LIFE,
WHAT YOU WILL EAT
OR DRINK; OR ABOUT
YOUR BODY, WHAT
YOU WILL WEAR.
IS NOT LIFE MORE
IMPORTANT THAN
FOOD, AND THE BODY
MORE IMPORTANT
THAN CLOTHES ?"

" LOOK AT THE BIRDS
OF THE AIR; THEY DO
NOT SOW OR REAP OR
STORE AWAY IN BARNS.
AND YET YOUR HEAVENLY
FATHER FEEDS THEM.
ARE YOU NOT MUCH
MORE VALUABLE THAN
THEY ?"

"W H O OF Y O U BY
42 21 31   44 31 37

W O R R Y I N G CAN ADD A
42 31 34 34 42 22 27 17

S I N G L E H O U R TO
35 22 27 35 15   31 43 31 34

HIS L I F E? AND W H Y DO
     15 22 16 15   42 31 44

VOU WONNY A B O U T
          11 32 31 43 17

C L O T H E S? SEE HOW THE
35 15 31 17 35 15 35

L I L I E S OF THE
15 22 15 22 15 35

F I E L D G R O W. THEY
16 22 15 15 34   31 34 31 42

DO NOT L A B O R OR
        15 11 32 31 34

S P I N."
35 32 27 27

MATTHEW 6:27-28

181

ABCDEFGHIJKLMNOPQRST
UVWXYZ

"<u>SO</u> <u>DO</u> <u>NOT</u> <u>WORRY</u>,
<u>SAYING</u>, '<u>WHAT</u>
<u>SHALL</u> <u>WE</u> <u>EAT</u>?' <u>OR</u>
'<u>WHAT</u> <u>SHALL</u> <u>WE</u>
<u>DRINK</u>?' <u>OR</u> '<u>WHAT</u>
<u>SHALL</u> <u>WE</u> <u>WEAR</u>?'"
"<u>DO</u> <u>NOT</u> <u>BE</u> <u>ANXIOUS</u>
<u>ABOUT</u> <u>ANYTHING</u>,
<u>BUT</u> <u>IN</u> <u>EVERY</u>-
<u>THING</u>, <u>BY</u> <u>PRAYER</u>
<u>AND</u> <u>PETITION</u>,
<u>WITH</u> <u>THANKS</u>-
<u>GIVING</u>, <u>PRESENT</u>
<u>YOUR</u> <u>REQUESTS</u> <u>TO</u>
<u>GOD</u>."

"<u>THERE</u> IS NO <u>FEAR</u> IN
<u>LOVE</u>. BUT <u>PERFECT</u>
<u>LOVE</u> <u>DRIVES</u> OUT FEAR.
<u>BECAUSE</u> <u>FEAR</u> HAS TO
DO WITH <u>PUNISHMENT</u>.
THE <u>ONE</u> WHO <u>FEARS</u> IS
<u>NOT</u> MADE <u>PERFECT</u> IN
<u>LOVE</u>."

1 JOHN 4:18

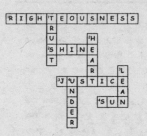

"<u>THOSE</u> WHO <u>KNOW</u>
36 21 31 15 15   24 27 31 42
YOUR <u>NAME</u> WILL <u>TRUST</u>
27 11 26 15   36 34 37 35 36
IN YOU, <u>FOR</u> <u>YOU</u>, LORD,
16 31 34   44 31 37
HAVE <u>NEVER</u>   <u>FOR</u>-
27 15 41 15 34   16 31 34
<u>SAKEN</u> THOSE <u>WHO</u>
35 11 24 15 27   42 21 31
<u>SEEK</u> <u>YOU</u>."
35 15 15 24   44 31 37

PSALM 9:10

"<u>IN</u> <u>YOU</u> <u>I</u> <u>TRUST</u>,
<u>O</u> <u>MY</u> <u>GOD</u>, <u>DO</u> <u>NOT</u>
<u>LET</u> <u>ME</u> <u>BE</u> <u>PUT</u>
<u>TO</u> <u>SHAME</u>, <u>NOR</u>
<u>LET</u> <u>MY</u> <u>ENEMIES</u>
<u>TRIUMPH</u> <u>OVER</u>
<u>ME</u>."

PSALM 25:2

1. <u>CHARIOTS</u>
   <u>HORSES</u> <u>NAME</u>

2. <u>TRUST</u>

3. <u>HEARTS</u> <u>REJOICE</u>
   <u>HOLY</u>

"DO NOT LET YOUR
HEARTS BE TROUBLED.
TRUST IN GOD; TRUST
ALSO IN ME. IN MY
FATHER'S HOUSE ARE
MANY ROOMS; IF IT
WERE NOT SO, I
WOULD HAVE TOLD
YOU. I AM GOING
THERE TO PREPARE
A PLACE FOR YOU.
AND IF I GO AND
PREPARE A PLACE
FOR YOU, I WILL
COME BACK AND TAKE
YOU TO BE WITH ME
THAT YOU ALSO MAY
BE WHERE I AM. YOU
KNOW THE WAY TO
THE PLACE WHERE I
AM GOING."

"MAY THE GOD OF HOPE FILL YOU WITH ALL JOY AND PEACE AS YOU TRUST IN HIM, SO THAT YOU MAY OVERFLOW WITH HOPE BY THE POWER OF THE HOLY SPIRIT."

ROMANS 15:13

A B C D E F G H I J K L M N O P Q R S T U V W X Y Z

"KEEP YOUR LIVES FREE FROM THE LOVE OF MONEY AND BE CONTENT WITH WHAT YOU HAVE, BECAUSE GOD HAS SAID, 'NEVER WILL I LEAVE YOU; NEVER WILL I FORSAKE YOU.'"

"FOR THE LOVE OF MONEY IS A ROOT OF ALL KINDS OF EVIL. SOME PEOPLE, EAGER FOR MONEY, HAVE WANDERED FROM THE FAITH AND PIERCED THEMSELVES WITH MANY GRIEFS."

1 TIMOTHY 6:10

"THEN HE SAID TO THEM, 'WATCH OUT! BE ON YOUR GUARD AGAINST ALL KINDS OF GREED; A MAN'S LIFE DOES NOT CONSIST IN THE ABUNDANCE OF HIS POSSESSIONS.'"

LUKE 12:15

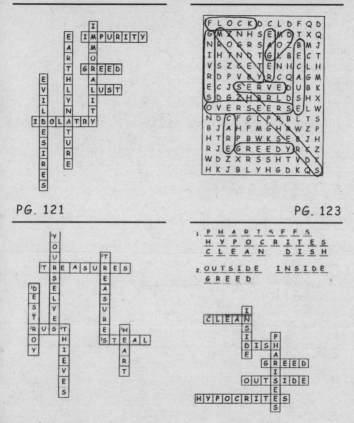

"TO THE MAN WHO
PLEASES HIM, GOD
GIVES WISDOM,
KNOWLEDGE AND
HAPPINESS, BUT
TO THE SINNER
HE GIVES THE
TASK OF GATHER-
ING AND STORING
UP WEALTH TO
HAND IT OVER TO
THE ONE WHO
PLEASES GOD.
THIS TOO IS
MEANINGLESS,
A CHASING AFTER
THE WIND."

ABCDEFGHIJKLMNOPQRST
UVWXYZ

"MOREOVER, WHEN
GOD GIVES ANY
MAN WEALTH AND
POSSESSIONS,
AND ENABLES
HIM TO ENJOY
THEM, TO ACCEPT
HIS LOT AND
BE HAPPY IN
HIS WORK — THIS
IS A GIFT OF
GOD."

"EACH ONE SHOULD
       31 27 15   35 21 31 31 37 25 14
USE WHATEVER
    42 21 11 36 15 41 15 34
GIFT HE HAS RE-
17 22 16 36   34 15
CEIVED TO SERVE
13 15 22 41 15 13   35 15 34 41 15
OTHERS, FAITHFULLY
31 36 21 15 34 35
ADMINISTERING
11 14 26 21 11 16 15 35 12 27 17
GOD'S GRACE IN ITS
      17 34 11 13 15
VARIOUS FORMS.
41 11 34 22 31 37 35   16 31 34 34 26 35
                        I PETER 4:10

186

" SING AND MAKE MUSIC
IN YOUR HEART TO THE
LORD . ALWAYS GIVING
THANKS TO GOD THE
FATHER FOR EVERYTHING ,
IN THE NAME OF OUR LORD
JESUS CHRIST ."

EPHESIANS 5:19-20

"TO Y O U , O L O R D , I
44 31 37   25 31 34 14
L I F T UP M Y S O U L ."
25 22 16 36   26 44 35 31 37 25

PSALM 25:1

" T U R N TO M E AND BE
36 37 34 27   26 15
G R A C I O U S   TO
17 34 11 13 22 31 37 35
ME , F O R I A M L O N E L Y
16 31 34   11 26 25 31 27 15 25 44
AND A F F L I C T E D ."
11 16 16 25 22 13 36 15 14

PSALM 25:16

1 P E A C E   S A F E T Y
2 G I V E S   B L E S S E S
P E O P L E
3 G O O D   S E E K
P U R S U E

187

ABCDEFGHIJKLMNOPQRST
UVWXYZ

"T H E R E F O R E,
S I N C E   W E   H A V E
B E E N   J U S T I F I E D
T H R O U G H   F A I T H,
W E   H A V E   P E A C E
W I T H   G O D   T H R O U G H
O U R   L O R D   J E S U S
C H R I S T."

"I F   I T   I S   P O S -
S I B L E,   A S   F A R
A S   I T   D E P E N D S
O N   Y O U,   L I V E   A T
P E A C E   W I T H
E V E R Y O N E."

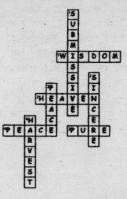

"LET THE _PEACE_ OF _CHRIST_
RULE IN YOUR _HEARTS_, SINCE
AS _MEMBERS_ OF ONE _BODY_
YOU WERE CALLED TO _PEACE_ ."
COLOSSIANS 3:15

"_FLEE_ THE EVIL _DESIRES_ OF
YOUTH, AND _PURSUE_
RIGHTEOUSNESS. FAITH,
LOVE AND _PEACE_, ALONG
WITH THOSE WHO CALL ON THE
LORD OUT OF A PURE _HEART_.
DON'T HAVE ANYTHING TO DO WITH
FOOLISH AND STUPID
ARGUMENTS, BECAUSE YOU
KNOW THEY PRODUCE _QUARRELS_ ."
2 TIMOTHY 2:22-23

188

"PEACE I LEAVE WITH YOU; MY PEACE I GIVE YOU. I DO NOT GIVE TO YOU AS THE WORLD GIVES. DO NOT LET YOUR HEARTS BE TROUBLED AND DO NOT BE AFRAID."

JOHN 14:27

"I HAVE TOLD YOU THESE THINGS, SO THAT IN ME YOU MAY HAVE PEACE. IN THIS WORLD YOU WILL HAVE TROUBLE. BUT TAKE HEART! I HAVE OVER-COME THE WORLD."

JOHN 16:33

"WHEN TEMPTED, NO ONE SHOULD SAY, 'GOD IS TEMPTING ME.' FOR GOD CANNOT BE TEMPTED BY EVIL, NOR DOES HE TEMPT ANYONE; BUT EACH ONE IS TEMPTED WHEN, BY HIS OWN EVIL DESIRE, HE IS DRAGGED AWAY AND ENTICED. THEN, AFTER DESIRE HAS CONCEIVED, IT GIVES BIRTH TO SIN; AND SIN, WHEN IT IS FULL-GROWN, GIVES BIRTH TO DEATH."

JAMES 1:13-15

189

MULTIPLE CHOICE

"PEOPLE WHO WANT TO GET RICH FALL INTO TEMPTATION AND A TRAP AND INTO MANY FOOLISH AND HARMFUL DESIRES THAT PLUNGE MEN INTO RUIN AND DESTRUCTION."
I TIMOTHY 6:9

AFTER READING THE VERSE ABOVE, WHAT WOULD BE THE RIGHT CHOICES BELOW?

1. YOU GET A LOT OF MONEY FOR YOUR BIRTH DAY.
   A) YOU HIDE IT AWAY, SO YOU DON'T EVER HAVE TO SHARE.
   B) YOU GIVE SOME BACK TO GOD, PUT SOME TOWARDS SAVINGS, AND TAKE A LITTLE TO SPEND.
   C) YOU SPEND IT ALL AT THE LOCAL VIDEO ARCADE.

2. YOUR YOUNGER BROTHER'S BIKE HAS A FLAT TIRE AND HE HAS NO MONEY TO REPAIR IT.
   A) YOU OFFER TO LOAN HIM THE MONEY AND HE CAN PAY IT BACK WHEN HE CAN.
   B) YOU TELL HIM TO TAKE CARE OF HIS OWN PROBLEMS.
   C) YOU GIVE HIM THE MONEY AS LONG AS HE CLEANS YOUR ROOM FOR THE NEXT YEAR.

3. YOU FINALLY GOT THAT NEW GAME SYSTEM!
   A) YOU SHARE IT WITH NO ONE.
   B) YOU SPEND ALL YOUR TIME AT IT... YOUR CHORES AREN'T GETTING DONE AND YOUR GRADES ARE SLIPPING.
   C) YOU CAREFULLY SCHEDULE YOUR TIME ON IT.

4. YOU'VE BEEN ASKED AT CHURCH TO GIVE TO AN EMERGENCY RELIEF FUND.
   A) YOU GIVE TEN PERCENT OF YOUR SAVINGS.
   B) YOU'RE ANGRY BUT GIVE BECAUSE IT IS EXPECTED OF YOU.
   C) YOU ASK GOD WHAT AMOUNT HE WOULD HAVE YOU GIVE.

A B C D E F G H I J K L M N O P Q R S T
U V W X Y Z

"BECAUSE HE HIMSELF SUFFERED WHEN HE WAS TEMPTED, HE IS ABLE TO HELP THOSE WHO ARE BEING TEMPTED."

"LET US THEN APPROACH THE THRONE OF GRACE WITH CONFIDENCE, SO THAT WE MAY RECEIVE MERCY AND FIND GRACE TO HELP US IN OUR TIME OF NEED."

"BROTHERS, IF SOMEONE IS CAUGHT IN A SIN, YOU WHO ARE SPIRITUAL SHOULD RESTORE HIM GENTLY. BUT WATCH YOURSELF, OR YOU ALSO MAY BE TEMPTED."
GALATIANS 6:1

PG. 163 crossword:

- B R O T H E R S
- S U F F E R I N G
- P R O P H E T S
- J O B S
- S E E N
- N A M E
- M E R C Y
- B L E S S E D
- P E R S E V E R E D

PG. 165 crossword:

- K I N D N E S S
- P A T I E N C E
- D I S C R E D I T E D
- S E R V A N T S
- E N D U R A N C E
- T R O U B L E S
- B E A T I N G
- H A R D S H I P S
- R I O T S
- P U R I T Y
- D I S T R E S S E S

"<u>B E A R</u> IN <u>M I N D</u> THAT
  12 15 11 34   16 22 27 14

OUR <u>L O R D' S</u> <u>P A-</u>
      15 31 14 14 35   22 11

<u>T I E N C E</u> MEANS <u>S A L-</u>
36 22 15 27 13 15   35 11 25

<u>V A T I O N</u>, JUST AS OUR
41 11 36 22 31 27

DEAR <u>B R O T H E R</u>
       12 34   31 36   21 15 34

<u>P A U L</u> ALSO <u>W R O T E</u>
32 11 37 25   42 34 31 36 15

YOU WITH THE <u>W I S D O M</u>
                   47 22 35 14 31 26

THAT <u>G O D</u> GAVE HIM."
       17 31 14

2 PETER 3:15

SUPER BIBLE ACTIVITIES FOR KIDS!

Barbour's Super Bible Activity Books, packed with fun illustrations and kid-friendly text, will appeal to children ages six to twelve. And the price—only $1.39—will appeal to parents. All books are paperbound. The unique size (4⅛" x 5⅜") makes these books easy to take anywhere!

A Great Selection to Satisfy All Kids!

Bible Activities

Bible Activities for Kids

Bible Connect the Dots

Bible Crosswords for Kids

Bible Picture Fun

Bible Word Games

Bible Word Searches for Kids

Clean Jokes for Kids

Fun Bible Trivia

Fun Bible Trivia 2

Great Bible Trivia for Kids

More Bible Activities

More Bible Crosswords for Kids

More Clean Jokes for Kids

Super Bible Activities

Super Bible Crosswords

Super Bible Word Searches

Super Silly Stories